60 DAYS OF FAITH FOR WOMEN

60 DAYS OF FAITH FOR WOMEN

A Devotional
to Deepen Gratitude,
Praise, and Prayer

Rev. Cameron Trimble

ROCKRIDGE
PRESS

Interior and Cover Designer: Peatra Jariya
Art Producer: Megan Baggott
Editors: David Lytle, Andrea Leptinsky, and Nicky Montalvo
Production Editor: Nora Milman

Illustration: BreckCreate/IStock

Author photo © Randy Fulford, 2019

ISBN: Print 978-1-64152-828-3 | eBook 978-1-64152-829-0

R0

To women

who trust

their power

to create a more

loving world.

CONTENTS

HOW TO USE THIS BOOK

I believe all of us are "in progress." We are growing, changing, evolving, and becoming. We can also regress, digress, and get lost on our way to knowing ourselves and God. These lessons rarely come from books themselves but from the questions they provoke. And such lessons often return to us throughout our life journey as our perspective changes.

Devotionals can help create space for you to enter into conversations with the Sacred. I certainly hope this book helps you do that. But I also hope it creates a conversation within you, encouraging you to discover more about your own soul and voice. For far too long, we women have questioned our own wisdom and wondered about our right to help shape our collective future. But we are now seeing a powerful resurgence of ancient, feminine wisdom that has been patiently waiting to be rediscovered in the lives of modern women and men.

The simplest way for you to use this book is to read one devotion per day for 60 days. You can start reading at any time of the year. I wrote each devotion in the hope that you would create for yourself a 60-day window for self-reflection and personal spiritual growth. Each devotion has reflection questions or exercises that help you go deeper in your own self-exploration inspired by the devotion of the day.

At the beginning of each chapter, you will find a Scripture reading that comes from the New Revised Standard Version of the Bible. This translation, published in 1989, benefits from the gains of hundreds of years of biblical scholarship and is considered by most biblical scholars to be the most accurate English translation to date. I hope you will also find that this translation has, for the most part, maintained much of the beautiful prose and poetry of the English language without sacrificing the accuracy of the original texts.

The heart of the devotions themselves are stories or parables I wrote to reflect both the Scripture and modern life. Theologian Karl Barth famously said that all Christians should approach the world with the newspaper in one hand and their Bible in the other. We gain deep wisdom when we view our world through the lens of a just and generous faith.

Stories often need a transport system from our ears to our minds and hearts. When they find their way to our hearts, they change us. I wrote the

reflection questions and exercises with that journey in mind, hoping that we might together embed these stories into the marrow of your bones. It's there that they truly come to life.

Some of the reflections are questions for you to consider. I've provided space for you to write out your thoughts as they come. Try not to censor or edit them in your head before you write them down. Your true intuition, God's still small voice that speaks to you, is often your first and clearest thought. I hope you learn to trust that voice as you write. Because these exercises are for you and you alone, I hope you find your way to writing with vulnerability and honesty. I've journaled for over 27 years and have found the practice to be life-changing.

Some of the reflections are guided meditations where I encourage you to go on an imaginative exploration within yourself. For these, read through the entire reflection exercise. When you are ready, close your eyes and simply begin with what you can remember. Don't obsess over getting every step I might have suggested. As you begin the journey, you may find yourself adding to the narrative. Go with it. Trust your instincts. Again, God may very well be leading you where you need to go. The most important part is simply beginning.

When you sense yourself ready to close your devotional time, read through the prayer at the end of each chapter. Sometimes I take a photo of the prayer on my phone so that I can carry it with me throughout the day. Prayers are a form of poetry—they are best savored.

As you read this book, you may decide that you would enjoy talking through some of the stories with friends—embrace that feeling. Consider inviting people to your home, reading one devotion together, and then talking about what wisdom it offered to you. With more conversation partners, you will see new insights you might have missed. You can conclude your time with the prayer at the end of the chapter.

If you are a member of a congregation, you might also find this book useful for classes or small group gatherings. While I am writing these with women in mind, these devotions apply to everyone. We all long to know love, to belong in a group, to relish adventure, and to know God.

I pray that the 60 devotions included in this book bring you new life. The Christian journey involves learning, growing, and expanding—and so do we. Gratefully, we are accompanied by a God who is with us always, still speaking words of hope and healing, as we move toward wholeness.

INTRODUCTION

I was 14 years old when I started reading devotionals. I would get up early in the morning before school and sit down at the old wooden desk in my bedroom. I would light the candle that sat on my desk close to the wall and spend a few moments in silence. When I felt "open," I would turn to my devotional book and start reading.

When I finished, I would open my journal. I would ask that God speak to me through my writing. I want to be clear: God has never spoken to me in an audible voice. But I do know something of that "still small voice" that the prophet Elijah talks about in 1 Kings 19:12. As I began to write, I had a clear sense of ideas and feelings flowing through me that were both of me and not of me. It was me writing the words on the page, but the flow, the wisdom, and the insight that came through my writing felt as if they had been mixed into a beautiful conversation with God. For me, at that age, it was healing magic.

Here is what I know of life so far in sitting with God. . . .

We have stories that live deep within our bones. They are ancient stories that make sense of the world through knowing that women, in particular, are gifted in sensing. The stories we carry speak to archetypal truths—realities described with words but that exist far beyond words—teaching us what is possible in ourselves and in the world.

We share similar dreams and desires. We want to know ourselves and know God. We want to feel alive and to know unconditional love. We want to do meaningful work. We want to have friends we can count on. We want to be less lonely, afraid, anxious, and stressed. We want to find balance and live a life of purpose. We want to matter.

I believe our world needs a global spiritual movement dedicated to an awakening that is twofold. We must wake up and rediscover the wisdom of our ancestors, the wonderful old storytellers who would sit by the fires and tell tales of hope and trials and transformation. We must also wake up to the ever-evolving realities of our world today—artificial intelligence, global commerce, social media, global migration, and a warming planet. We need wisdom bearers now more than ever, who can help us all create a world that works for everyone and is shaped by kindness, generosity, and sacrificial love. My hope, in the end, is that we shape a world that looks, acts, and talks like Jesus.

Being a pilot as well as a pastor has taught me about altitude and perspective. Flying at 3,000 feet, I can see cars and houses, how neighborhoods connect, and where urban areas become suburban. At 32,000 feet, I can see our horizon and what feels like endless land stretched out before me. All of this beauty was here all along, but I needed to change altitudes to be able to see it.

When life stops making sense for me individually or for us collectively, I've learned that changing altitudes or vantage points helps me see life differently. It gives me a new perspective to consider as I learn more about all of God's creation. The practice of reading daily devotions, writing in my journal, and praying helps me make that shift. God always teaches me something new by showing me truths that have been there all along, but I couldn't yet see them. In this way, the path of wisdom, at least for me, comes from trusting that God is always speaking, always revealing new truths and insights, and always leading us to new heights in our faith journeys.

Faith is an ever-evolving and expanding journey of coming to know ourselves and God. Like any religion, our Christian faith should draw us to each other and challenge us to love more fully and generously. The Bible teaches us that we are all God's children—we belong to each other because we belong to God.

My hope for this devotional book is that we are all reminded of our limitless capacity for love. I also hope that we are challenged to awaken even more to our own strength, creativity, courage, and shared vision for "heaven on earth."

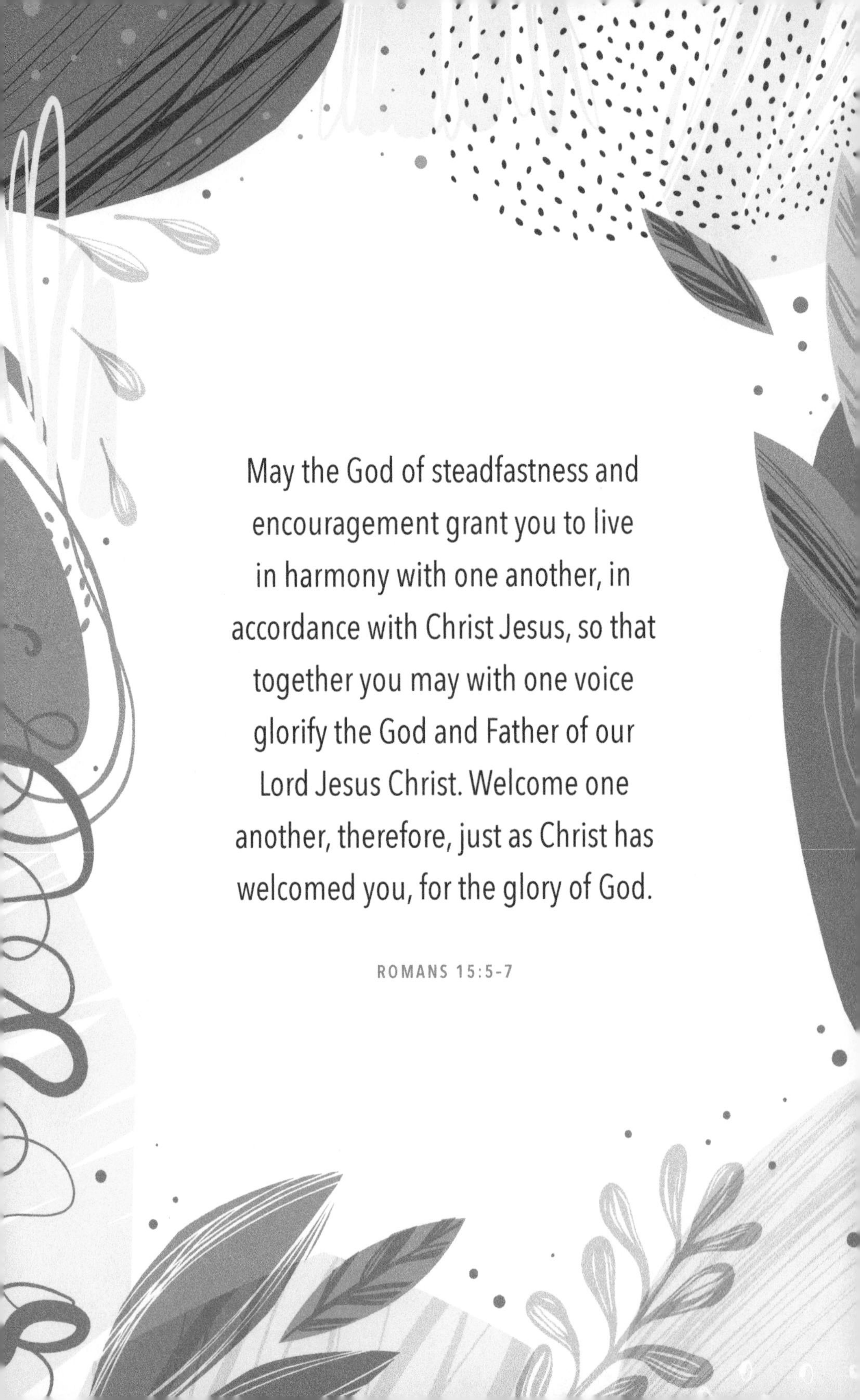

May the God of steadfastness and encouragement grant you to live in harmony with one another, in accordance with Christ Jesus, so that together you may with one voice glorify the God and Father of our Lord Jesus Christ. Welcome one another, therefore, just as Christ has welcomed you, for the glory of God.

ROMANS 15:5-7

WE'VE BEEN WAITING FOR YOU

Recently, I heard a beautiful story from a friend about her experience hiking the El Camino de Santiago in Spain with her father. To complete this walk, you need many weeks, and you walk dozens of miles a day. It's rigorous and transformative for those who take on the challenge. One afternoon, she and her dad stopped in a pub along the way to get food. The pub was packed full of people; there wasn't an empty table in the place. As they searched, they spotted a table with two people sitting there and two empty seats. She went over to ask them if she and her dad could join them. Without hesitation, the man sitting at the table said, "We've been waiting for you."

She said to me, in reflection, "That greeting made all of the difference for us. We didn't feel like we had to beg for a place at their table, as if we were inconveniencing them. We felt an immediate welcome, as if we belonged and could share the space together."

The most important gift we give to one another is a sense of belonging and connection. With loneliness and isolation becoming a crisis of our age, what if we began saying, "We've been waiting for you" to our new neighbors who move in? Or to a new employee on our team or new parents at our children's school? Or to our new daughter-in-law to welcome her into the family?

The Apostle Paul reminds us that we are built for a relationship with God and with each other. Jesus was the great model for this kind of generous community. He taught us that God doesn't force us into a relationship but waits for us to come, welcoming us with unconditional love and grace. We are therefore called to welcome others with a generosity that makes them feel seen, heard, and safe.

When we find new people to welcome in, let's remember that we've been waiting for them—and tell them so. Of course, they've been waiting for us, too.

REFLECT

Think about an upcoming event or project that is making you anxious. Maybe you are joining a new book club or making a presentation to a new client. Perhaps you're moving into a new neighborhood. What makes this experience feel scary?

What would be different if you believed that those you will meet have been waiting for you as if you were a long-lost friend?

CLOSING PRAYER

God of Grace,
In every season,
In every moment,
May I find your presence
calling me more fully into myself.
Remembering,
I am your beloved child.
You are waiting for me. Always.
Amen.

For surely I know the plans
I have for you, says the
Lord, plans for your welfare
and not for harm, to give
you a future with hope.

JEREMIAH 29:11, NRSV

WHEN LIFE TAKES A TURN

Caroline, a member of my congregation, checked her e-mail just before leaving for the office on Monday morning. That was how she discovered that she and her colleagues had just been laid off. The e-mail told her to stay home, and they would mail her personal belongings from her desk to the home address they had on file. They also thanked her for her 12 years of service.

Shocked would be an understatement of how Caroline felt in receiving this news. And it quickly shifted to anger and then became anxiety. What would she do next? Who was she without that job? What did this mean for her future?

As the days turned into weeks and Caroline went to dozens of job interviews, she felt something slowly awakening in her and began to sense a new kind of creative energy bubbling up in her spirit. She would often get an offer after her interviews, but none felt right.

One morning, she went on a walk through the center of her town. In the window of a storefront was a small decorative sign that said:

"Sometimes you have to let go of the picture of what you thought life would be like and learn to find joy in the story you are living."

She reflected later that reading that sign set her free. She asked some challenging questions of herself about the kind of life she wanted to live, and then she took the steps to make it happen. In her case, Caroline found her calling by working with troubled teens in a summer Outward Bound program. She knew she would never work an office job again.

I believe God designed all of life to be *for* us. The world is designed in a God-centered, God-patterned way that hopes for our wholeness and works for our happiness. Our role is to be open to the adventures that will come. The prophet Jeremiah reminds us that we can trust that God is working to give us a future with hope.

I pray this day you embrace the joy of the story you are living—or you decide to live a better story.

REFLECT

When you think about the twists and turns of your own life, what has surprised you about the journey?

If you imagined yourself in your 90s writing a letter to yourself today, what advice and wisdom would you offer?

You are the light of the world. A city built on a hill cannot be hid. No one after lighting a lamp puts it under the bushel basket, but on the lampstand, and it gives light to all in the house. In the same way, let your light shine before others, so that they may see your good works and give glory to your Father in heaven.

MATTHEW 5:14–16

THE TRAGEDY OF AN UNUSED GIFT

When I was a very young child, I went to Six Flags Over Georgia one day with my family and walked into one of those stores that sells the little glass figurines. I was entranced—all of those little statues were so beautiful and delicate that I almost felt like I shouldn't breathe in case I knocked one over. As I was browsing, I came across a little figurine of a horse that captured my heart. I grew up riding horses and to this day love them, so I decided to buy that little horse with my allowance money and take him home.

The salesclerk put it in a little white box, and for the rest of the day, I didn't go on any other rides. I just held my little box so that no one would sit on it or do anything to break it. When I got it home, I pulled it out and looked at it for at least an hour. But then I decided to put it right back into that box because I was sure that if I left it out, it would be broken.

And there that little horse lay for 10 years. I completely forgot that I even had it, and I never enjoyed its beauty that had captured me that first day. I never let others see its intricate patterns carved into the tail and mane. I never offered it as a gift to someone who also might love it like I did in that moment. I kept it hidden and protected so that nothing bad would ever happen to it.

As I was going through my possessions as an adult, I found my little horse in that box. But that box had been put under a larger, heavier box, so that when I opened it, I discovered that the horse that I had so thoughtfully protected had been crushed.

I learned something important that day. Anytime you receive something precious, you have to make a decision. Either you can share that gift with yourself and others, or you can hide it away. I hid my little horse and denied myself and others the beauty it was designed to shine into the world.

You *are* that gift. God created you as a gift to the rest of us. Jesus tells us in Matthew's Gospel that God created you to be a light that shines brightly, illuminating the rest of us with your presence. That means that you have to risk being snuffed out or broken. We are all robbed of your gift if you close yourself off and hide away. That is the one thing you can't do. God needs you to show up and show out. Actually, we all do.

REFLECT

When you think about your family, what gifts do have that you sometimes hold back from them? What would change if you risked offering them?

Consider the three most important people in your life. They might be coworkers, your family, or your friends. What gifts do they have that you have seen them try to hide? How could you invite them to risk sharing them?

CLOSING PRAYER

Gracious God,
Grant me the courage to risk sharing what feels precious, to offer to others what I hold as valuable. May I also be humble enough to receive the gifts that others offer to me, seeing your love and grace in them.
Amen.

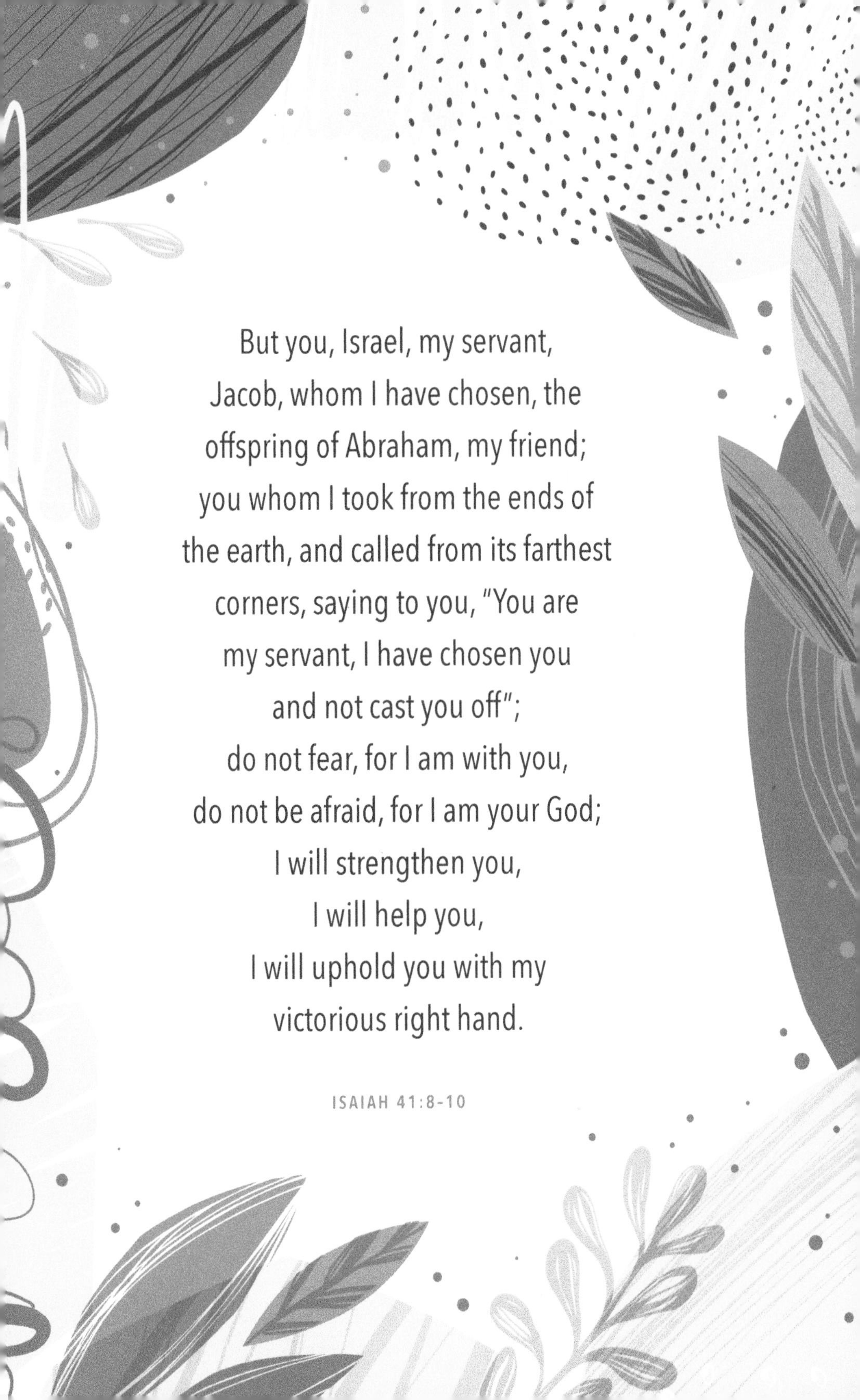

But you, Israel, my servant,
Jacob, whom I have chosen, the
offspring of Abraham, my friend;
you whom I took from the ends of
the earth, and called from its farthest
corners, saying to you, "You are
my servant, I have chosen you
and not cast you off";
do not fear, for I am with you,
do not be afraid, for I am your God;
I will strengthen you,
I will help you,
I will uphold you with my
victorious right hand.

ISAIAH 41:8-10

DISCOVERING RESILIENCE

Each of us has lived through moments of heartbreak. Perhaps you lost a child or a partner. Maybe you were fired from a job, or your home burned and you lost possessions that you valued. Possibly a friend betrayed you, or you experienced divorce. You might have had the experience of being discriminated against. Maybe you have been unjustly persecuted.

We all share the pain of heartbreak. It's part of what unites us as spiritual beings having a human experience.

It's interesting what we choose to do in response. Does the experience shape us, or do we shape it? Resilient people face heartbreak with relentless hope in a better future. None of us want to suffer or experience pain. But some of us know that it's in the crucifying experiences of life that resurrection comes.

This passage from Isaiah is one of my favorites because it reminds us of why we need never be afraid: God is with us. No matter what happens, no matter how we fail, no matter how we succeed, God reminds us that he will be there for us through it all.

If you are facing tough days, know you are not alone. If you're not, give thanks and love those people in your life who are. We are all in this together, and God is with us.

REFLECT

Consider your most challenging time in life—a time when you were not sure if you would succeed or survive or persevere. What were your greatest fears in those moments? What gave you courage? What gift did the experience give you that you can now recognize as you look back?

Now think about your experience of God in that challenging time. Did God feel near to you, or did he feel far away? Does reading Isaiah 41 help you see ways that God has been with you all along?

When the Pharisees heard that he had silenced the Sadducees, they gathered together, and one of them, a lawyer, asked him a question to test him. "Teacher, which commandment in the law is the greatest?" He said to him, "'You shall love the Lord your God with all your heart, and with all your soul, and with all your mind.' This is the greatest and first commandment. And a second is like it: 'You shall love your neighbor as yourself.' On these two commandments hang all the law and the prophets."

MATTHEW 22:34-40

HOW TO FIND PEACE

Jesus provided us with a clue to living at peace when he gave us the great commandments. He said that we are to first love God with our heart, then with our soul, and then with our mind. Our starting place for accessing God is through our heart, not our head. Our trouble is that most of the time, we get that backward.

In his autobiography, the psychologist Carl Jung, one of the great explorers of the inner life, described a conversation he had with a Native American chief named Mountain Lake, whom he regarded as a kindred spirit. "I was able to talk to him as I have rarely been able to talk to a European," Jung recalled. Perhaps because of their mutual respect, Mountain Lake gave Jung a very frank assessment of the way his people saw Europeans.

"Their eyes have a staring expression," the chief said. "They are always seeking something. What are they seeking? The whites always want something. They are always uneasy and restless. We do not know what they want. We do not understand them. We think they are all mad."

Jung asked Chief Mountain Lake to elaborate: Why, exactly, did white people seem so insane to the Native Americans?

"They say they think with their heads," responded Mountain Lake.

"Why, of course," said Jung. "What do you think with?"

"We think here," said Chief Mountain Lake, and he pointed to his heart.

Perhaps you have experienced Chief Mountain Lake's wisdom in your own life. Women often lead with our hearts, trusting our inner intuition as much as we trust our logical minds. In this way, we can use all of the ways of connecting with the wisdom within us. It's that integration of head, heart, and soul that allows us to connect most deeply with God. When we love with every part of us, we can then *love our neighbors as ourselves.* When we love God and one another, we find peace within us and between us. It's simple, but it's not easy.

REFLECT

Sit quietly and close your eyes. Take five deep breaths. Then invite yourself as a young girl to become present with you. Ask that young girl what she wants for herself. What makes her happy? What makes her feel at peace? What makes her feel safe but not stifled?

Now invite your 90-year-old self to be present with you. Ask her the same questions. What do you imagine she wishes for herself? What makes her happy? What makes her feel at peace? What makes her feel safe but not stifled?

Do your younger self and your older self say similar or different things?

CLOSING PRAYER

Lord, make me an instrument
of your peace;
where there is hatred, let me sow love;
where there is injury, pardon;
where there is doubt, faith;
where there is despair, hope;
where there is darkness, light;
and where there is sadness, joy.
—St. Francis of Assisi

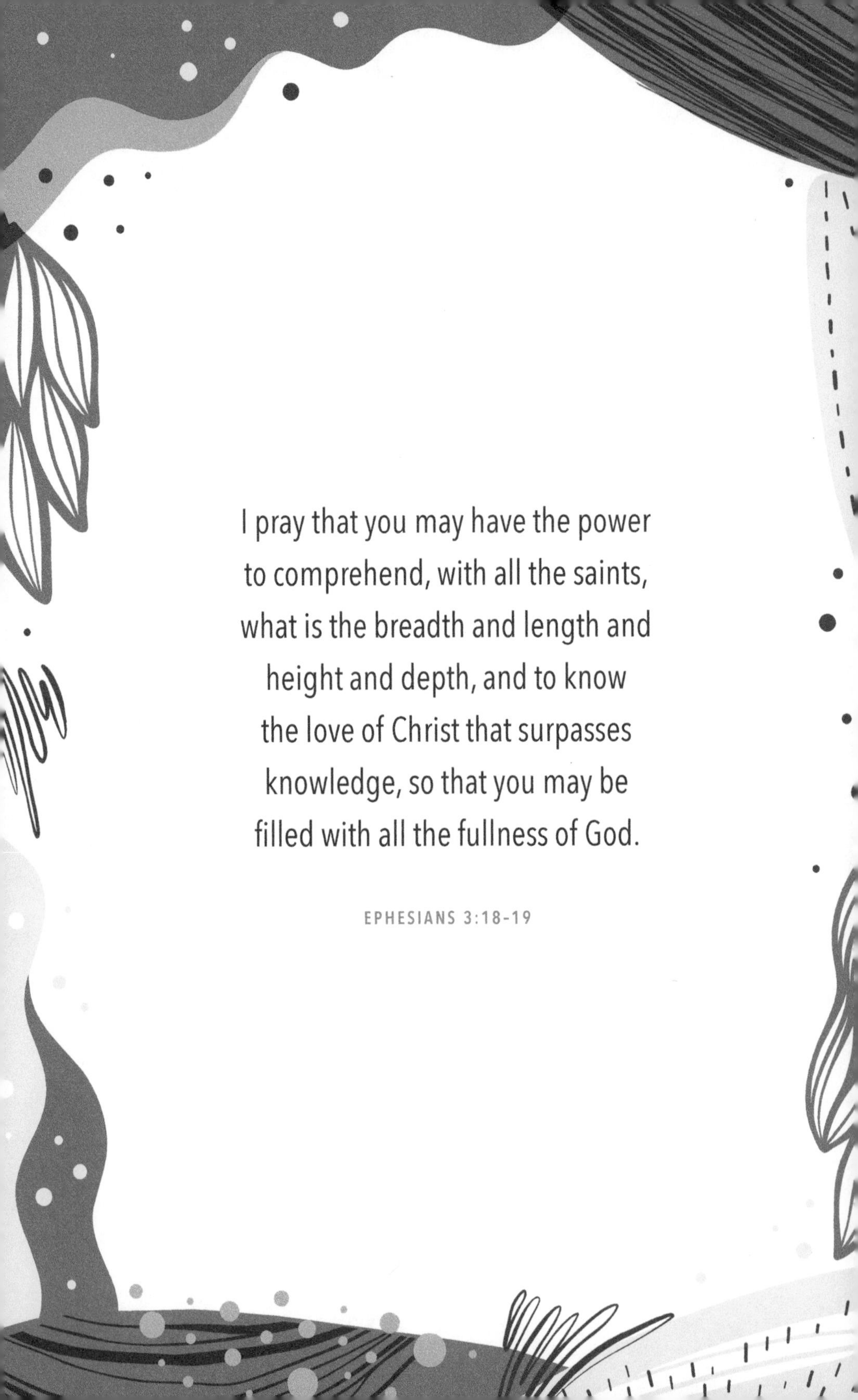

I pray that you may have the power
to comprehend, with all the saints,
what is the breadth and length and
height and depth, and to know
the love of Christ that surpasses
knowledge, so that you may be
filled with all the fullness of God.

EPHESIANS 3:18-19

MY MOTHER ALWAYS DID THIS

Jim and Carol were excited to spend their first Christmas together as newlyweds. This would be Carol's first Christmas meal she prepared with Jim serving as sous chef. After unwrapping the meat and setting it on the cutting board, Carol chopped off both ends of the ham with a butcher knife and tossed the two small ends in the garbage can.

"Wait a minute," said Jim, a little mystified. "Why did you do that? Why did you just cut off the ends of the ham like that?"

"I don't know. My mother always did," Carol answered. "Maybe it helps bring out the flavor."

Unsatisfied with this answer, Jim called his mother-in-law and asked, "Can you tell me why you cut the two ends off a ham before you cook it?"

"Well," said the mother-in-law, "I'm not really sure why. That's just the way my mother did her ham, and it was always delicious."

As soon as Jim hung up, he called Carol's grandmother and asked her, "Grandma, we have an important question for you. Can you tell us why you cut the ends off of a ham before you cook it?"

"Oh my, yes, dear," answered Grandma in her quiet voice. "I have a pan that has never quite been big enough, so I cut the ends off to make it fit."

Every one of us is shaped by traditions and ways of seeing the world that have been passed down to us from generations that have come before. Often those lessons keep us safe, healthy, and happy. But sometimes they serve no purpose at all, and we end up "throwing out the ends of the ham" without knowing why.

The life of faith is one that requires that we maintain our curiosity. Carol would still be cutting the ends off her hams if Jim hadn't thought to ask why she was doing that. The only way we will ever know *"the breadth and length and height and depth, and to know the love of Christ that surpasses knowledge"* is to stay curious about how God is transforming us and our world today. We can't always assume that what we were taught is always right. God may be ready to teach you something new. When we are open to learning, we are filled with the fullness of God.

REFLECT

Write about an experience of doing something that your mother or grandmother taught you, but you have no idea why you did it. Does it still serve you today?

What belief did you hold about God when you were younger that has changed over time?

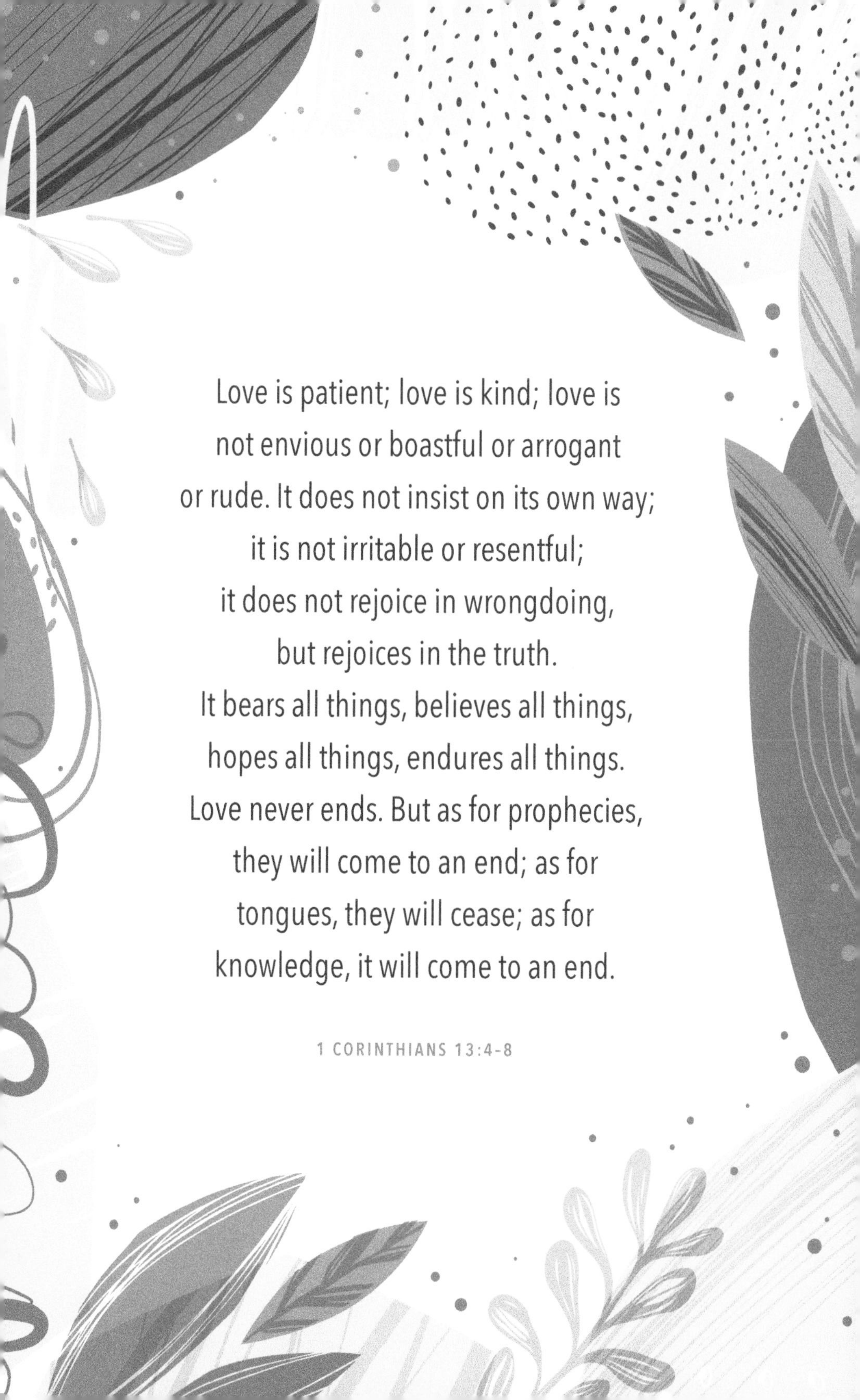

Love is patient; love is kind; love is
not envious or boastful or arrogant
or rude. It does not insist on its own way;
it is not irritable or resentful;
it does not rejoice in wrongdoing,
but rejoices in the truth.
It bears all things, believes all things,
hopes all things, endures all things.
Love never ends. But as for prophecies,
they will come to an end; as for
tongues, they will cease; as for
knowledge, it will come to an end.

1 CORINTHIANS 13:4-8

MY FAVORITE LOVE STORY

One Sunday during my sermon, I read one of my favorite stories to the congregation. It is a book written by Robert Munsch called *Love You Forever*. It tells of a mother who watches her son grow up through the years, longing to express the incredible love that all good parents feel for their children. She holds him in her arms as a baby, rocking him back and forth, and sings a beautiful lullaby to him about how much she loves him.

As the boy grows into a toddler and then a teenager and then finally an adult, she continues to hold him and rock him back and forth, back and forth, singing her song of love.

Finally, when she is old and tired, she calls her son to come visit her. She tries to sing her lullaby to him, but she is too weak to finish it. Hearing her struggle, her son goes to her, picks her up into his lap, and sings it back to her.

I don't think there is anything as sacred as having someone who loves us deeply sing or pray for us—it unleashes a Spirit that speaks possibility into our lives like nothing else.

1 Corinthians is a favorite text for most of us because it reminds us that God's essence (and therefore ours) is love. We are created to love. We need to love. It's what we are on this earth to do. And to do that, we have to practice being patient, kind, generous, and compassionate with each other. Over the years of life together, we become more like God.

Jesus's prayer was finally that we would know God as surely as we know ourselves. But the good news is that regardless, God will always be singing the lullaby of unconditional love in the earnest hope that we one day sing it back.

REFLECT

Think about someone in your life who embodied the kind of love that 1 Corinthians talks about—a love for others that is patient, kind, generous, and compassionate. How do you think they became that way? What can you learn about your own life by looking at theirs?

CLOSING PRAYER

Loving God,
Make me an instrument of your love,
that I might be
patient
kind
generous
compassionate
in all things,
toward all people,
for all my days.
Amen.

Put away from you all bitterness
and wrath and anger and wrangling
and slander, together with all
malice, and be kind to one another,
tenderhearted, forgiving one another,
as God in Christ has forgiven you.

EPHESIANS 4:31-32

WHAT YOU WISH TO SEE

As a mother, I worry about children living in a world that isn't kind or fair. I want to work to make it better for them—for all of us. To begin that work, I needed to learn about the journeys of others. I wanted to know what causes the pain that makes them lash out in anger. I wanted to know what oppresses them and holds them back. I wanted to know what dreams they hold and where they hope they will go in life.

By having conversations with people who are different from me, I began to learn a new vocabulary. I learned about words like *micro-aggression*. According to Dictionary.com, the term was first used in 1970 to mean a comment or action that subtly and often unconsciously or unintentionally expresses a prejudiced attitude toward a member of a marginalized group.

As I learned more about the journeys and stories of people who are different from me, I became more curious. I started to pay attention to the ways I responded with kindness and used my influence. I considered what others were experiencing on a daily basis that I didn't experience because of my skin color and economic status. Soon, I began to wonder if there was an antidote to microaggressions.

During a recent business trip to New York City, as aggressive as the city is perceived to be, I was deeply touched and at times overwhelmed by the acts of kindness and inclusion that I witnessed.

- The woman on the train who gave five dollars to the teenager who said he was hungry.
- The man in the meeting who corrected his client for talking over his female colleague.
- The white woman who declined her boss's assignment and instead nominated her Iranian colleague to take the lead in a major presentation.
- The young man who helped an elderly woman push her cart across the intersection.
- The Uber driver who was delayed picking me up because his last ride was a blind man who needed help up the stairs to his apartment.

Every time I turned around, I witnessed people caring for one another in ways that acknowledged their privilege and also showed deep kindness.

Could it be that some of us—more than we think—are becoming more sensitive to one another's needs and wanting to help make life just a bit easier for each other? If so, I have hope for our nation and our world.

God longs for us to live at peace with one another and to treat each other with the deepest kindness we can offer. We can do that only when we treat each other with respect, honor that we are all God's children, and love one another as God in Christ has loved us. We all love each other imperfectly at times. We often need to ask one another for forgiveness. But Ephesians says to keep trying. Love one another, forgive one another, hold one another accountable, and try again.

I've always been struck when I read stories of Jesus as he faced tough questions and hostile acts from people who were out to harm him. In the face of the worst persecution, Jesus stood up for the most vulnerable, showing compassion for those in need. Maybe that is happening to us, too.

REFLECT

What acts of kindness have you seen these past few days that surprised and inspired you?

How might you be more sensitive to different people's experiences?

Do not be conformed to this world, but be transformed by the renewing of your minds, so that you may discern what is the will of God—what is good and acceptable and perfect.

ROMANS 12:2

DO NOT BE CONFORMED TO THIS WORLD

"If you want to stand on a stage as a public speaker, you need to lose some weight," my advisor told me. I instantly felt shamed, my face blushing. I thought my weight was okay. My body isn't built to be tiny, but still, I felt guilty for taking up too much space in the world. I'm right at the line of healthy body mass, according to our culture. But apparently, on a stage, the lights must put additional weight on me.

I tried to reframe his comments in my mind by saying, "You need to be committed to health, Cameron. As long as you are eating right and exercising, you are doing what you can. That's all you can do." But his comment made a mark. It echoed in the back of my mind. I was fat, and everyone could see it. If I wanted to continue to speak in churches or conferences, I needed to drop some pounds to be attractive.

So I did. I conformed. I dropped 10 pounds. I admit it felt good, until I opened the refrigerator door every day and beat myself up for what I should and should not eat. It became a daily battle of discipline and will. Some days I would fail.

I imagine body image is a challenge that all women face. Do you struggle with the pressure to dress in a way others will find attractive, even if it doesn't feel right on your body? How do you let other people's opinions determine what you embrace and enjoy about yourself?

Romans 12:2 becomes a liberating verse when we consider that the "ways of the world" are not always God's will. Our social pressures and definitions of "attractive" and "unattractive" are human constructs, not anything that God would ever impose on us. As one who has made the mistake of conforming to the trends of the world, I can tell you they're not worth obsessing over. We are good and holy and beautiful in God's sight because we are made in God's image. We are enough, and we always have been.

When you feel pressured by messages from others to be or do something that doesn't feel authentic to you, remember these words from Romans: God has given you your life to live; no one else deserves the right to live it for you.

REFLECT

What messages do you tell yourself about your body that are positive and affirming? What messages do you tell yourself that are negative and hurtful?

What wisdom would God offer you about knowing what is beautiful about being you?

CLOSING PRAYER

Gracious God,
Remind me that my beauty should never be defined by the latest trends or public opinion. I am an expression of you, holy and sacred and made in your image. Help me discover the deep sense of comfort that comes when I am no longer influenced by others, when I can look within myself and see that marvel that you created in me.
Then I will be free.
Amen.

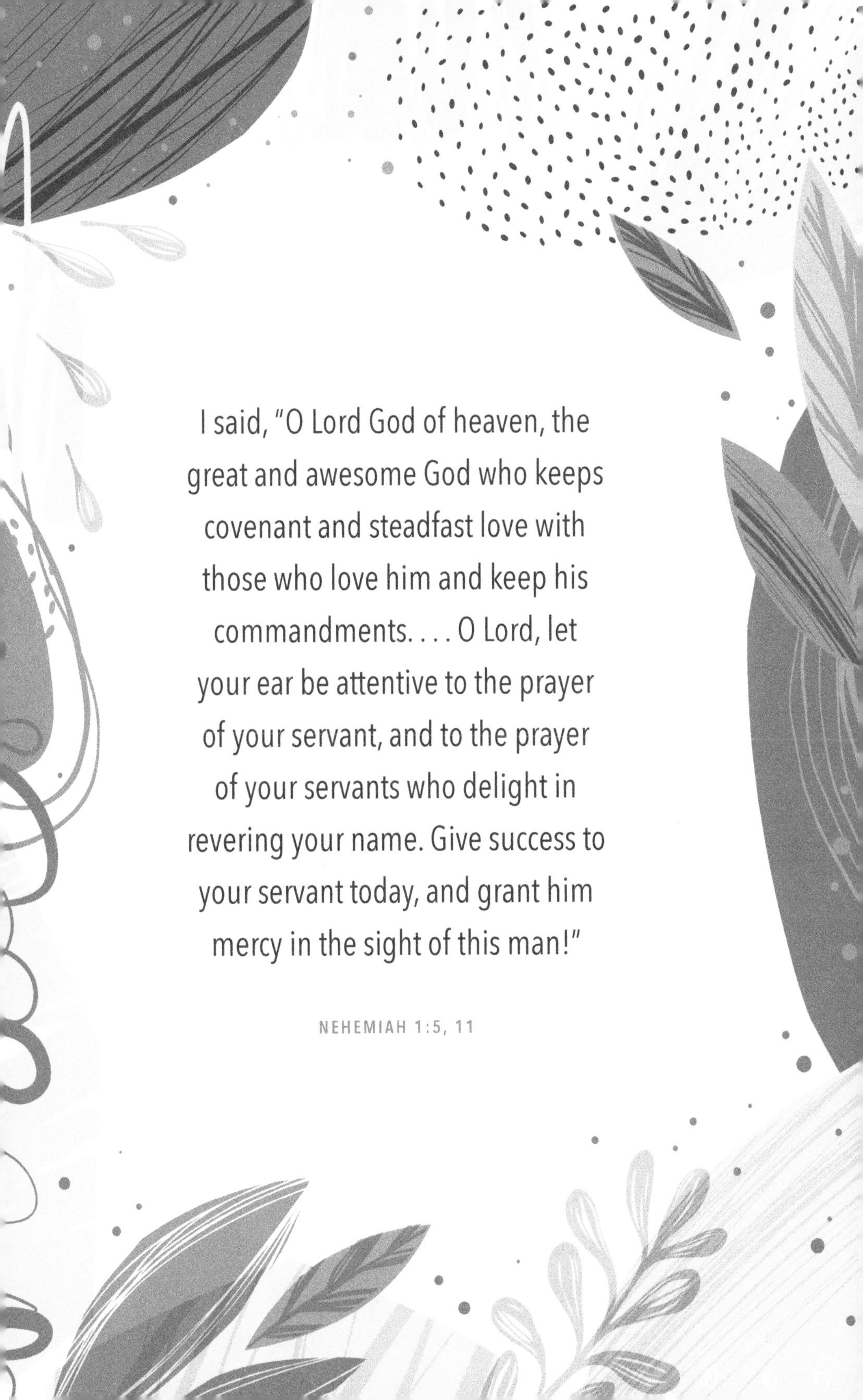

I said, "O Lord God of heaven, the great and awesome God who keeps covenant and steadfast love with those who love him and keep his commandments. . . . O Lord, let your ear be attentive to the prayer of your servant, and to the prayer of your servants who delight in revering your name. Give success to your servant today, and grant him mercy in the sight of this man!"

NEHEMIAH 1:5, 11

YOUR CAPACITY TO DREAM

Nehemiah is one of my favorite characters in Scripture. He is just a regular guy who sees brokenness in the world and decides he is going to do something about it. In his case, he sees that the walls of Jerusalem have been torn down. These walls represent the pride of his people. But unlike everyone else who can see that the walls lie in ruins, Nehemiah decides he is going to rebuild them, not for his benefit or profit but for the sake of his people. He has a huge vision for what is possible and is willing to take the risks to make it so. We can learn from that.

When people hear that I am a pilot, they make the assumption that I enjoy taking risks. I am not risk-averse, but I am not crazy either. In fact, flying has made me take fewer risks because, in an airplane, there is more at stake.

Flying has taught me endless lessons, but perhaps the most important one is about scale and vision. Our capacity to dream has everything to do with our courage to expand our vision.

The world looks different when you see it from the ground or 3,000, 14,000, or 32,000 feet. Your perspective changes. The conditions change. The kind of aircraft you need to safely traverse the airspace changes. Your sense of your own skills changes. The way you see yourself in the world changes. With each new altitude, you learn something essential about yourself and about the world.

Real adventure is seeking new altitudes, seeing the world from different perspectives. The wider your view, the less risky new adventures feel to you. The hardest part, the step that requires the most courage, is simply getting into the plane in the first place.

Sometimes it's hard to see large visions for our lives in isolation. I will often ask a small group of friends to gather at my home, and we take an evening to help each other dream about our lives. I might say, "What could I do in this coming year that would be bold and fun and make a difference?" Then they would start brainstorming ideas. We would do this for everyone in the group. It's a powerful practice if you have people you trust enough to call on for this exercise.

REFLECT

When have you felt yourself take on a risky vision for an exciting future?

What is the biggest dream you have for your life?

Then the Lord answered
me and said:
Write the vision; make it
plain on tablets, so that
a runner may read it.

HABAKKUK 2:2

RIGHT UNDER YOUR NOSE

Early in my flight training, I had to complete a cross-country flight with an instructor, James, using all manual calculations and a paper map. I carefully calculated my fuel burn for takeoff, landing, and each leg of the flight and marked points on the map that I should be able to see at specific times in the flight. As James and I took off, I tracked every minute of that flight on my map.

"I should see a cell tower to my left, eleven o'clock." Check.

"I should see smokestacks to my one o'clock in two minutes." Check.

Everything was going beautifully, and 45 minutes into the flight, I excitedly announced: "Here we are!" Then I looked out my windshield and couldn't see the airport anywhere. I looked to my left, scanning the houses, road, fields, but no airport. I rechecked my instruments and my map—the airport should have been right there. My mind raced—what had I done wrong?

James sat silently until it became clear that I wasn't going to figure this one out on my own. Then he leaned forward and said, "Look under your nose." I looked, and there was the airport, directly under the nose of my plane.

We miss important things in life when they aren't directly in our line of vision. We can make things far more complicated than is needed most of the time. Then we miss seeing what is right in front of us.

I learned an important lesson that day in my plane. When you are looking for what you need and can't find it, it's often right under your nose.

REFLECT

Lots of us struggle to see a clear "vision" for our life. Often I find it helpful to simply look for the "next best step." What might be your "next best step" as you navigate your day?

Having James in the plane was essential to helping me see where I was in my flight. He could see what I could not see. Who might be helpful to you as you move forward?

CLOSING PRAYER

Gracious God,
Give me the eyes to see and the ears to hear your vision and voice in my life. Then give me the courage to embrace your leading, knowing that you are always hoping for my wholeness.
Amen.

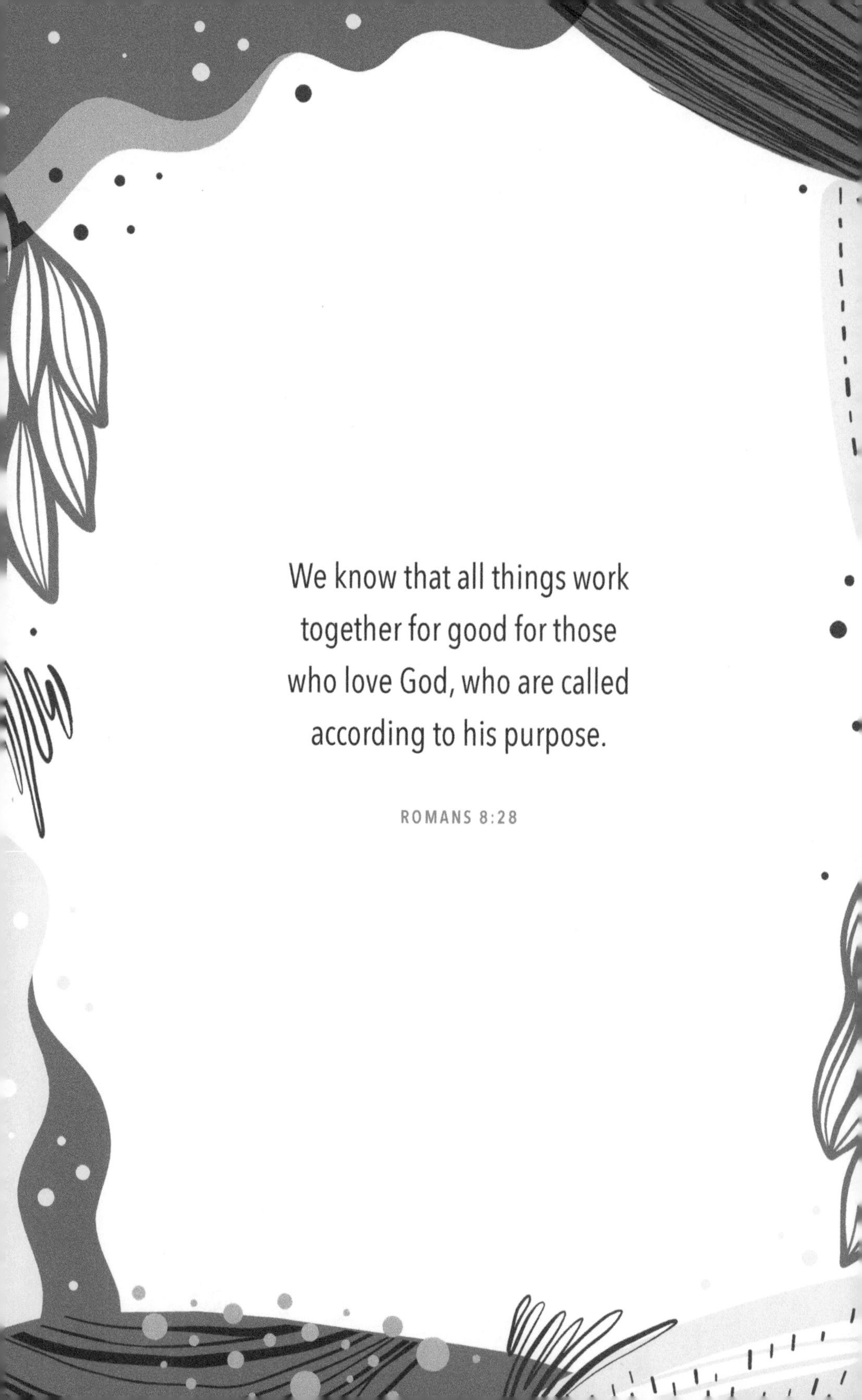

We know that all things work
together for good for those
who love God, who are called
according to his purpose.

ROMANS 8:28

WHAT IS YOUR LIFE PURPOSE?

Like most people, I have spent an inordinate amount of time trying to discern what God might wish me to make of my life. I have prayed, searched, talked, listened, probed, looked high and low, all in the hopes that I would find my one great calling. I grew up in churches where I heard sermons about "God's will for my life" and "finding my purpose-driven life." These left me as a child thinking that there was one great thing I was supposed to do with my life, and that my job was to figure out what that thing might be.

Finding this task to be frustrating, I made promises to God like "If you just tell me who I am supposed to be and what I am supposed to do, I promise I will behave." Today, I am incredibly grateful God never answered that particular prayer. As the saying goes, "Well-behaved women rarely make history."

What I know now is that finding purpose and vision for our lives is a process that can have any number of excellent endpoints. The prophet Jeremiah tells us that God works for our benefit (our welfare) and not for our harm. Our job is to move forward with hope. We can do lots of wonderful things with our lives that would be holy and pleasing to God. What God asks is not that we find the formula for the perfect life but that we open ourselves to the richness and joy of living in the ambiguity of blazing our own unique trail.

At the end of the day, life purpose is a very simple thing. It is the joining of your passion with the world's need. There are any number of ways to live your purpose. The question is: What makes you come alive?

REFLECT

Fill in the following statements:

When I was little, I wanted to be ______________________

when I grew up.

If it weren't such a crazy idea, I would really love to

____.

I feel most alive when ______________________________.

When I have free time, I love to spend it doing ____________

______________________________.

Do you see any themes or patterns? What has been true about you since you were little and is still true for you today? I find that God often guides us over time with a still small voice that keeps saying the same thing. We just have to learn how to hear it.

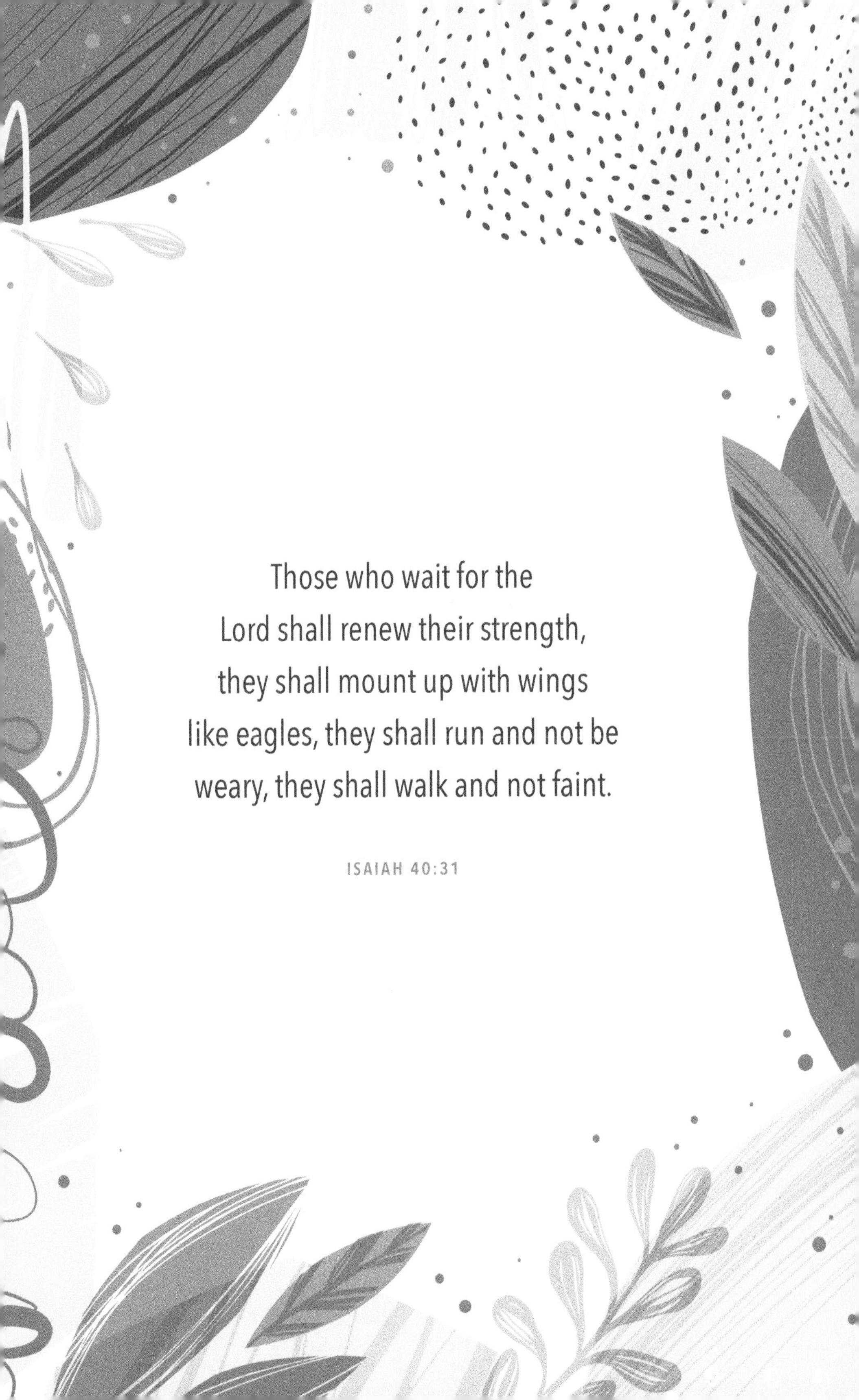

Those who wait for the
Lord shall renew their strength,
they shall mount up with wings
like eagles, they shall run and not be
weary, they shall walk and not faint.

ISAIAH 40:31

WHEN OTHERS BELIEVE IN US

My CrossFit coach is a tall, buff bald guy named Kevin who has 1 percent body fat and the perfect physique. There are many reasons why he is a fantastic coach, but what sold me is that he is actually in shape. He has achieved what I painstakingly strive for in myself.

Kevin always greets me at the gym, and we get started with the warm-up. I'm usually miserable and out of breath by the end. Then we move to stretching, my personal favorite, since I enjoy lying around extending my limbs like a lazy cat. I usually try to distract Kevin at this point so that we spend more time than planned on this.

Then we get to the actual workout. It tends to involve terrible, often unspeakable exercises like burpees and box jumps. I complain, loudly, to see if we can skip those. Most of the time, I lose.

During the workout, my brain starts yelling things at me:

- "Are you insane? You are a middle-aged woman! You do not need to be throwing your body on the floor over and over just to burn calories and stay strong."
- "You can't do this. You shouldn't even try. Who do you think you are?"
- "Everyone else in this class is way thinner and way younger. And besides, you don't jump."

But the greatest gift is that Kevin is yelling louder, telling me that I *can* do it. He believes beyond a doubt that I am making progress. And at that moment when I want to give up and die, it's Kevin who keeps me in the game.

1 Thessalonians 5:11 must be the Scripture for CrossFit coaches. Thank God, literally, Kevin has perfected it.

We all need a coach like Kevin. We need people who care about our goals, push us beyond our self-limiting beliefs, and refuse to give up on us. There are moments in life when we need to borrow someone else's confidence in us. That is the gift of the beloved community. We keep going because others believe we can.

REFLECT

Who is your Kevin, the person who pushes you to do more than you ever thought you could and brings out the best in you?

How are you encouraging others in your life to become more than they dreamed they could?

CLOSING PRAYER

Gracious God,
I am grateful that people come into
my life who see potential in me that
I often miss in myself. It's like they
see a glimpse of what you hope
I will also see one day. Thank you
for blessing my life with people who
build me up. I pray that I may do
that for them as well.
Amen.

Nicodemus said to him, "How can anyone be born after having grown old? Can one enter a second time into the mother's womb and be born?" Jesus answered, "Very truly, I tell you, no one can enter the kingdom of God without being born of water and Spirit. What is born of the flesh is flesh, and what is born of the Spirit is spirit."

JOHN 3:4-6

ARE YOU BORN AGAIN?

Are you a "born-again" Christian? For me, my answer depends on what you mean by that question.

Jimmy Carter first made that phrase so popular—and so confusing. During his presidency, Carter often referred to himself as "a born-again Christian," which was a new expression for most of us. What he was trying to say was that he encountered God's grace and love in a new way later in his life and was thereby transformed into a new creation. If we had left it with that definition, we would be in a better place. But the term has been used loosely throughout the years, in some cases inaccurately and in too many instances judgmentally.

What does it mean to be born again? To be born again is simply to be reconciled to God. Jesus might just as easily have said to Nicodemus, "You must experience and accept God's forgiving love." The expression *born again* is another way of saying just that. Further, every Christian has been born again. To speak of born-again Christians is to imply that there are some Christians who have not been born again. In some instances, unfortunately, the term is used arrogantly to suggest that members of certain groups are authentic, genuine Christians while people who are not members of that group are somehow illegitimate or counterfeit Christians. I don't believe this to be true.

The original Greek word ἀναγεννάω, which means "born again," has a dual meaning. It does mean born again in the sense of physically experiencing a second birth. This was what confused Nicodemus when he asked, "Can a person enter a second time into his mother's womb and be born?" Of course, that is not what Jesus was talking about. He was talking about a different kind of birth. Our first birth is a physical birth; our second birth is a spiritual birth. Jesus said, "That which is born of flesh is flesh. That which is born of the Spirit is spirit." This means, then, that the second meaning for *born again* is being born from above, being born from God. Being born with the eyes to see as God sees.

Mother Teresa was one of the best examples I know of this. When asked by a reporter how she could continue year after year to care for the poor and dying, to deal with the constant smell of poverty and threat of disease, she said simply, "When I look into their faces, I see the face of Jesus." She was born from above.

REFLECT

What does it mean to be born with the eyes to see as God sees?

When God looks at you, what do you think he sees?

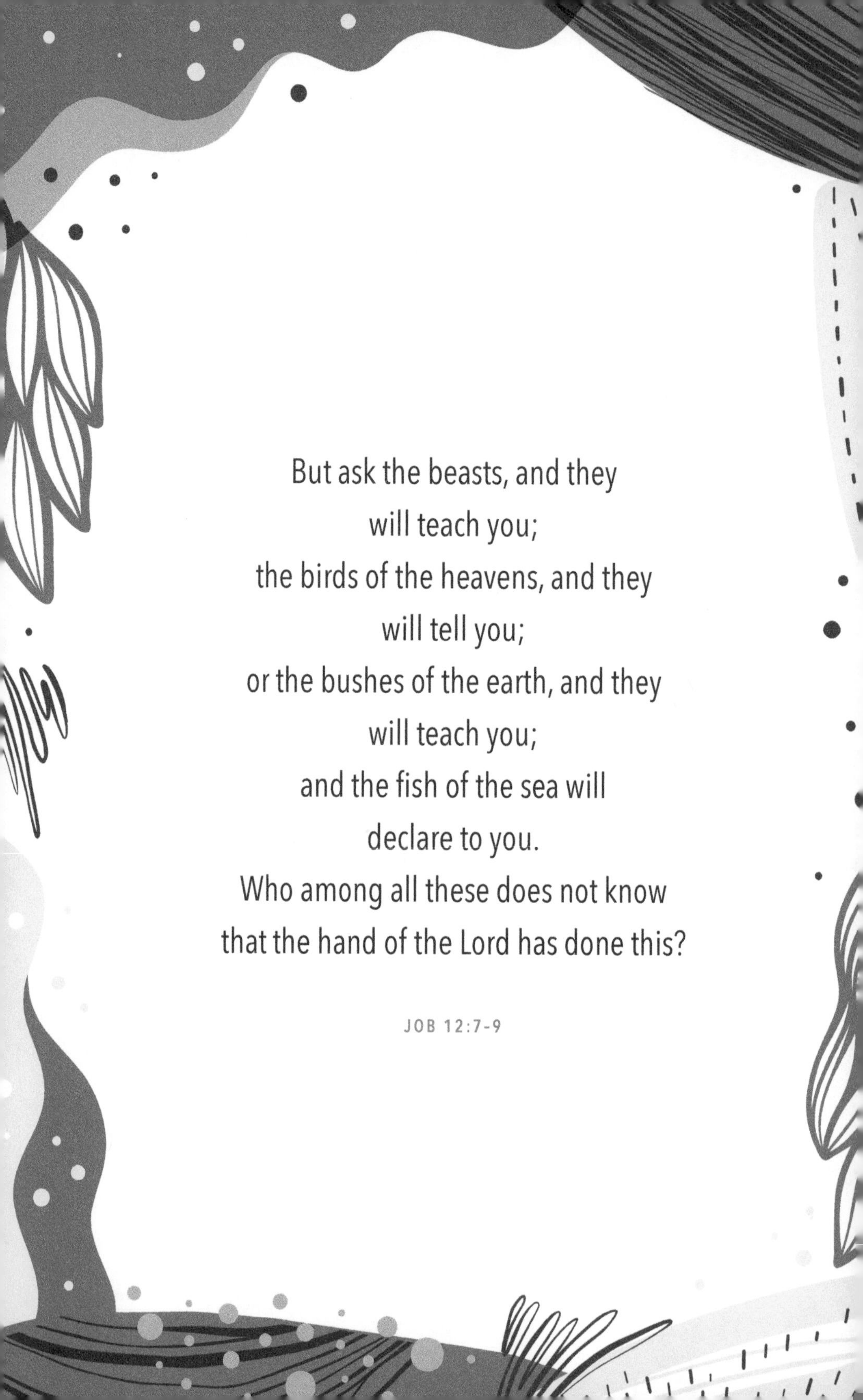

But ask the beasts, and they
will teach you;
the birds of the heavens, and they
will tell you;
or the bushes of the earth, and they
will teach you;
and the fish of the sea will
declare to you.
Who among all these does not know
that the hand of the Lord has done this?

JOB 12:7-9

CARE FOR OUR COMMON HOME

What if the planet is designed by God for our thriving? What if animals can teach us how to live in peace? What if plants actually care about our health because it is tied to their own? What if God wants us to care for creation because it's one more place that we can learn about God?

On May 24, 2015, Pope Francis published an encyclical called *Laudato Si*, with the subtitle *On Care for Our Common Home*. In it, he asks us to see the world as our shared home that we all have a responsibility to care for. His primary concern is that we can't cause harm to our planet in the pursuit of short-term material gains when it means we damage the planet in ways that hurt all of creation.

The Bible is full of reminders that we are all part of God's creation—the land and the sea, the birds of the air, the fish in the oceans, the plants and bees. Everything can teach us of God because everything comes from God. I especially love the passage from Job, a man who has gone through terrible trials and has been let down by friends, family, and his community. He needs a new way out of his suffering and hits upon the idea to ask the animals, the birds of the air, the plants of the earth, and the fish of the sea what is true and right.

Women throughout history have had a close, often mystical connection to nature. In many communities, women are the healers, knowing the plants that heal the wounds of their people. When we need to reconnect with ourselves, we often go on walks in the woods. We listen to the plants. We commune with the birds. We sense the energy of our planet in the core of our being.

Unfortunately, we collectively continue to cause such terrible harm to the planet. But God's invitation in this passage is to reconnect with our larger ecosystem when we need to reconnect with our truest selves. God says to listen to the wisdom of the plants, who can teach us once again about balance, healing, and living together in harmony.

REFLECT

Take a moment to look at a flower today. Notice its colors, the variations of shades that adorn its petals. Feel the stiffness or softness of its stalk between your fingers. What does it smell like? Sit with the flower long enough that you get a deep sense of it. Then consider what this flower can teach you about the world and about yourself.

CLOSING PRAYER

Creator God,
You made a beautiful world and called it good. You designed it to work for every living creature, adorned by your wild creativity and full of color, texture, smells, and sights. You called us to tend to this world, to get to know its beauty as an expression of yourself. Give us the wisdom to rediscover this beautiful world as if for the first time and to seek to live in balance with the plants and animals whose lives make our own possible.
Amen.

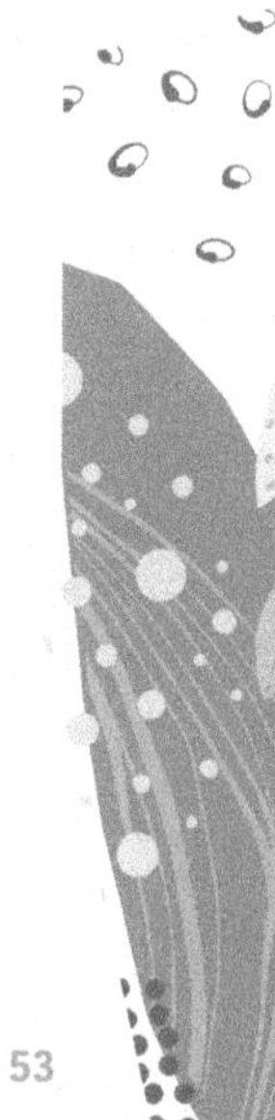

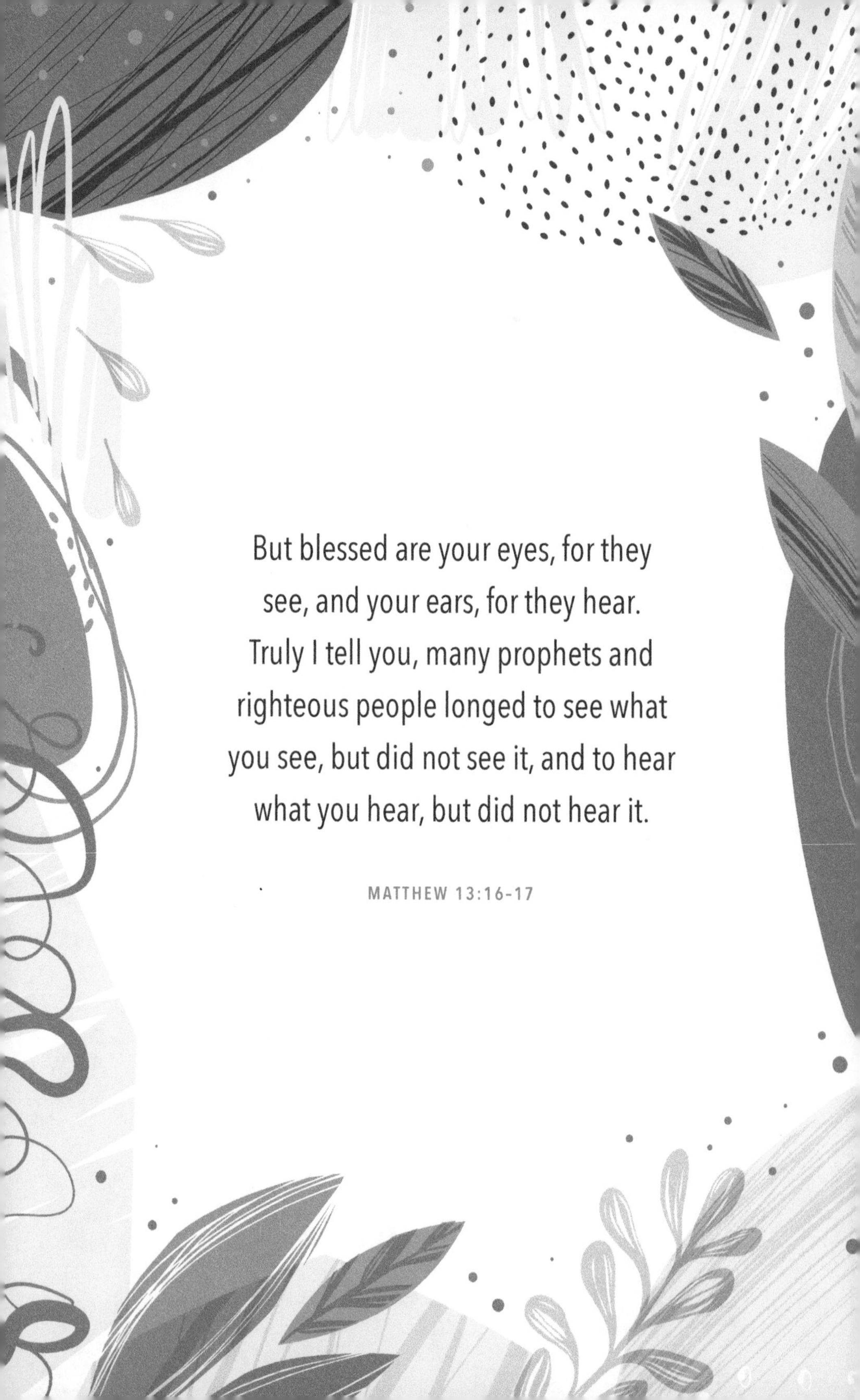

But blessed are your eyes, for they see, and your ears, for they hear. Truly I tell you, many prophets and righteous people longed to see what you see, but did not see it, and to hear what you hear, but did not hear it.

MATTHEW 13:16-17

HEARING GOD IN THIN PLACES

Spending time in a *thin place*—a place where you could sense God as more present than normal—on the Isle of Iona in Scotland has made me wonder about revelation. I've spent many hours there just being still, listening for that "still small voice," and I have been surprised by the experience. Even in the most beautiful place you can imagine, you can miss hearing the whisper of the Spirit. I've learned that what you focus on also determines what you miss.

I often lament that we are so overstimulated by our screens that we fail to look up and see the real world. But in Iona, you become overstimulated by the real world—the waves, the birds, the stunning green moss that grows on the rocks by the sea. You can become overwhelmed by the blue of the water and the wind that threatens to carry you away. The gift of a thin place, I now understand, is that its beauty breaks you open—shocks you into awareness and steals your breath—and then you have to step back into yourself, quiet your mind, and still your body simply to breathe.

That is when the inbreaking of God's voice happens. While you are catching your breath from the beauty before you, you are open to sensing sacred energy. Encountering a thin place, a place that wakes you up to God's presence through its sheer beauty, is a gateway to revelation about yourself, our beautiful world, and our endlessly loving God.

The stories of people encountering God in the Scriptures usually tell of unexpected encounters. People were going about their business, and then suddenly—BAM!—God or an angel appeared before them and spoke. The critical part comes next: They listened. Revelation is possible only in relationship. God speaks, and a person listens. Or maybe even a person speaks, and God listens?

I've never experienced God speaking to me in a booming voice or appearing to me in a way that makes me stop and say, "Hey, that's God!" But I have often had experiences with people or our planet that leave me certain that something of God was just revealed to me. I often hear God's love in a kind word spoken by a friend and sense God's sacred energy in the flow of a stream while I am on a hike. I see God's reflection in the face of a child and become enveloped in God's grace when my son hugs me. I might learn a bit more about love or grace or courage or kindness. I then usually have the sense that I am finally seeing what has been there all along.

Jesus once praised his disciples by saying, "Blessed are your eyes, for they see, and your ears, for they hear." It's not easy to hear the whisper of the Spirit these days, but I strongly encourage us all to try.

REFLECT

Who in your life has taught you to see God?

Have you ever encountered a "thin place"? Write about that experience.

As he approached the gate of the town, a man who had died was being carried out. He was his mother's only son, and she was a widow; and with her was a large crowd from the town. When the Lord saw her, he had compassion for her and said to her, "Do not weep."

LUKE 7:12-13

HELPING HIM CRY

Mrs. Minter's first-grade class was learning about kindness. She asked parents and students to notice when others were kind and then submit those stories for a contest at the end of the semester. Ellen, a mother of a child in the class, submitted a story about her son.

They had visited a nursing home the weekend before. Her son walked down the hall and came to an older man sitting in his room. He went in and talked to him for a while. Then he crawled into his lap and put his arm around the man's shoulder, patting him softly. About 10 minutes later, he crawled out of the man's lap and rejoined his mom. She asked what he and the older man had talked about. He said, "He was sad. All of his friends have died, and he misses them. I told him that I would be his friend so he wouldn't be lonely anymore."

Each one of us is hurting in some way. We may be struggling with a spouse who doesn't see us, children who rebel against us, a sense of inadequacy in ourselves, the loss of a friend or parent, the failure of a project, or the rejection of a friend. We are all grieving and all in the process of healing. This is the flow of life—life, death, life again.

We need each other in this process of grieving and healing. I often think how sad it is that we have turned our greeting question of "How are you?" into a common and meaningless form of superficial connection. We all respond as if by rote by saying, "I'm fine. How about you?" I wonder if we would know what to say if someone said, "I'm not good today." A response from the heart. A response that was true and honest and real. Would you run, or would you sit by them, hold their hand, and help them cry?

The Gospel writers note many times when Jesus was filled with compassion for the people. He faced their pain and helped in the ways he could. Let's follow his lead.

REFLECT

Sit quietly for a few moments. If you are comfortable, close your eyes. Then ask yourself, "Where do I hurt?" Feel the pain without feeding it. Offer the places you hurt compassion, like the little boy who put his arm around the old man.

CLOSING PRAYER

Loving God,
Sometimes I can look at someone and see their pain. I can see their loneliness and feel their sadness. Sometimes I look in the mirror and see those things in me. Help me not turn away or ignore what I or others are really feeling. Give me patience to sit with my neighbors as they navigate their pain, and help me welcome their accompaniment as I navigate my own. Through it all, help us all remember that we are not alone. You are with us always.
Amen.

For by grace you have been
saved through faith, and this is
not your own doing; it is the gift
of God—not the result of works,
so that no one may boast.

EPHESIANS 2:8-9

ENCOURAGEMENT FOR THE HOPELESS

Recently, I was on a work trip with the leaders of a fantastic church in San Diego. I sat in the restaurant of the hotel grabbing dinner before I went back to my room, and I soon realized I was in for a treat. In the middle of the restaurant, there were dozens of easels and canvases with people sitting patiently in front of them. I was suddenly in the middle of a "sip and paint" class.

The woman leading the session started by showing everyone the final picture that they would be creating together. She held up a canvas with a beautiful sunset between two hillsides. The colors were bold and blended perfectly, capturing those final glorious moments before the sun slipped below the horizon. Everyone looked at the finished work with a sense of awe and a twinge of excitement.

They all set to work on their canvases, but as I looked at the paintings that these people were creating, I wondered if we had seen the same sample painting only minutes before. Every participant seemed to have their own interpretation of the original task at hand, and some showed more talent than others.

One man started painting his sunset green. Another woman kept adding colors so that it looked like an off-color rainbow was dripping down her canvas. Another guy kept blending his colors down the canvas so that the entire thing became brown.

I watched as the instructor made her rounds, giving tips to those painting the canvases that were slightly salvageable. She offered generous words of encouragement to the ones that were hopeless. "You're doing a great job of moving the brush across the canvas," she would say.

In watching this scene in front of me, I was reminded that this is a beautiful example of living by faith. We don't get life right every time. We mess up. We hurt each other, usually by accident. But we keep trying because we know that God offers us forgiveness and grace. As Ephesians 2:8–9 tells us, we are saved by faith, not works. We are saved by trying, even if we fail. That night I learned that perfection isn't the goal. Just picking up the brush and moving it across the canvas is enough.

REFLECT

Write about a time when you tried something new, failed miserably, but had fun in the process. What did you learn about being playful and risking imperfection?

When did you learn that God never asks for perfection from you? What became possible for you when you finally accepted that gift?

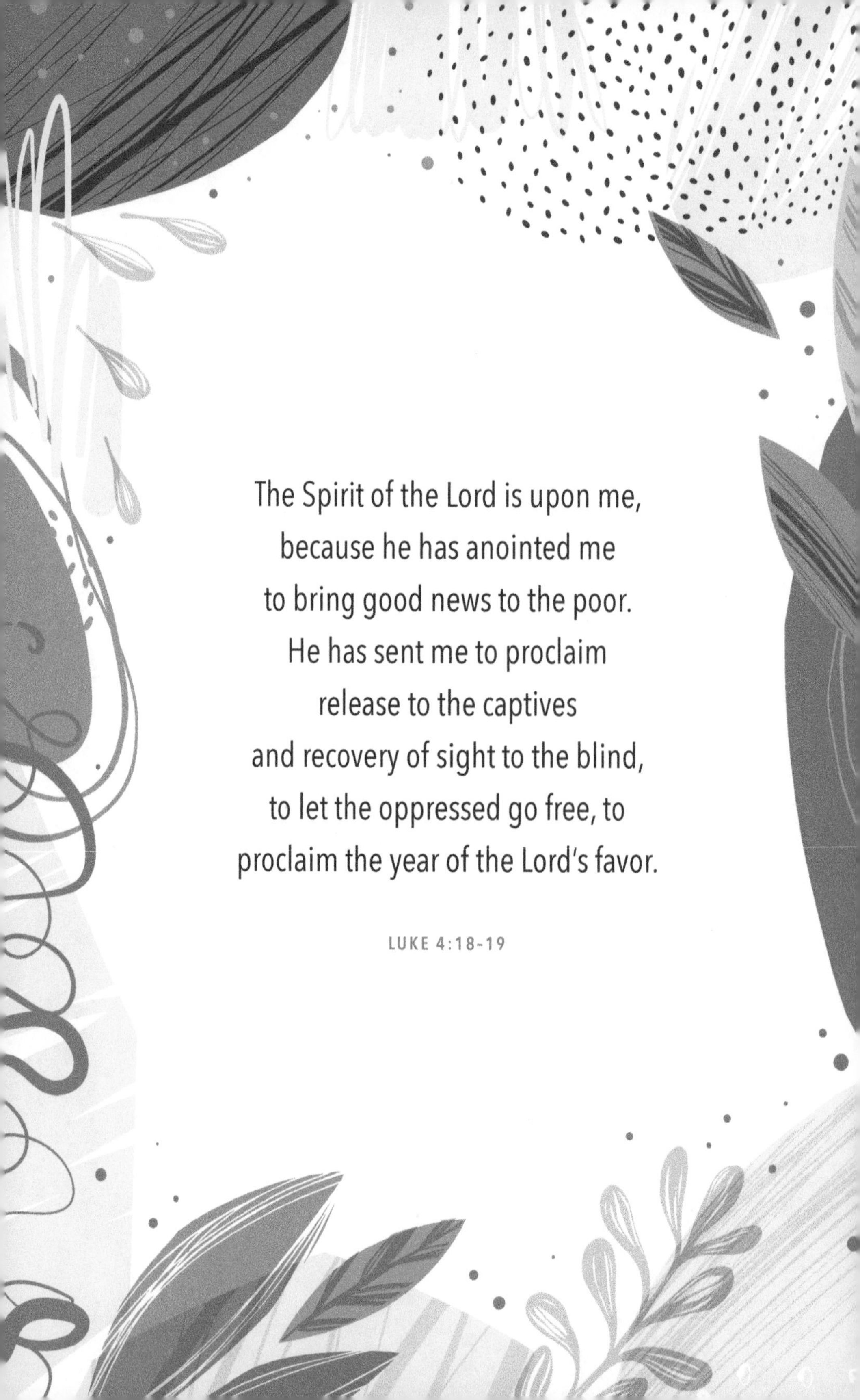

The Spirit of the Lord is upon me,
because he has anointed me
to bring good news to the poor.
He has sent me to proclaim
release to the captives
and recovery of sight to the blind,
to let the oppressed go free, to
proclaim the year of the Lord's favor.

LUKE 4:18-19

BLIND TO CHANGE

Blindness is a major theme in our Scriptures. The prophets talk about people not seeing God moving among them. Jesus used parables to help people see God and talked about people having the "eyes to see." In this passage in Luke, he tells people that he has come to help us recover our sight so that we can be set free to see as God sees.

I recently learned a new phrase: *change blindness*. It describes a perceptual phenomenon that occurs when a change in a visual stimulus is introduced and the observer does not notice it. You might experience this when you are looking for a friend in a crowded place. You scan the people standing around you and miss seeing her, even though she is standing right in front of you. Or you search for the cursor on your computer screen but can spot it only when you move your mouse. The movement catches your attention, even though the cursor was there all along.

We miss seeing a lot in life because of change blindness.

Some of us miss seeing our spouse grow lonely because we are absorbed by our phone at dinner. We miss hearing our kids tell us about their day because our ears are tuned in to the television. We miss checking in with aging parents because we are busy playing a game on our iPad.

I find myself wondering, what am I missing while I am being overstimulated by our modern life?

Jesus went to Nazareth one time and visited the temple. When he stood up to read, he was handed the scroll of the prophet Isaiah. Unrolling the scroll, he found the place where it talked about blindness and then went on to say that he came to be among us as a visible sign of God's presence and love with us. We were blind to that, and he came to recover the sight of the blind.

Because of this story in Luke, I now recognize my own deep longing to heal my change blindness. I want to live with my eyes and heart open to this beautiful and brutal world unfolding around me. Let's try together.

REFLECT

Sometimes we "blind" ourselves on purpose. We bury ourselves in our screens. We work too much. We watch television instead of talking to our families. We drink. How are you creating "blindness" in yourself? How does or doesn't that serve you?

What do you wish God would reveal to you that you can sense but cannot yet see? You may not have clear words or images. You may just be able to access impressions. Take a moment to explore that within yourself. What did you learn?

CLOSING PRAYER

In the midst of our familiar life, with
the people and places we see every day,
wake us up, O God, to see them with
fresh eyes. Let us see their joy and
their pain. Let us see their love and
their loneliness. And, in seeing it,
let us not turn away.
Amen.

Humble yourselves therefore under the mighty hand of God, so that he may exalt you in due time. Cast all your anxiety on him, because he cares for you. . . . And after you have suffered for a little while, the God of all grace, who has called you to his eternal glory in Christ, will himself restore, support, strengthen, and establish you.

1 PETER 5:6-7, 10

UNINTENTIONAL CRASH-LANDINGS

I went flying in my airplane over the weekend. About 30 minutes after I landed, a single-engine plane with retractable landing gear came in to land on the same runway. As I watched the plane descend, I realized that the left side wheel had failed to deploy correctly. I suspect the pilot of the plane already knew this. Planes have indicator lights that tell us if the landing gear is locked and active.

The plane landed on the right-side tire, then the nose wheel, and then collapsed to the left side, skidding to a stop. To the pilot's credit, he was on the centerline and exited the plane through the right passenger door. He nailed a textbook emergency landing. Everyone was okay. But every other pilot at the field that day had the color drain from their face—this was one of a list of experiences we would all rather not have.

Life is full of these, isn't it? We are all faced with challenging circumstances that test our skills, our patience, our wisdom, and sometimes our integrity. The key in these situations is being ready.

Here is what I do when I find myself in scary situations in life. I imagine three scenarios:

- What is the worst thing that could happen?
- What is the best thing that could happen?
- What can I live with?

Then I aim for the best possible outcome. In aviation, we are trained relentlessly to be prepared for these experiences. In life, well, it's hit or miss.

I don't believe that God sends suffering to us to teach us lessons. I do believe that God teaches us lessons while we're suffering. Life is full of challenges, most of which are created by humans. What God promises is that when we are deep in our anxiety, he cares about us and is with us in it. I find that to be enormously comforting.

As you imagine your future, think about the ways you want to grow, even if you have to risk suffering. Are there ways that you could intentionally challenge yourself to "level up"? Maybe you want to live with greater integrity. Maybe you want to face and conquer a fear that is holding you back. Maybe you want to find a job that uses your best skills. Maybe you want to be more present for your kids.

Whatever your "leveling up" looks like, go for it with all of your heart. Aim for the best possible landing. God is with you.

REFLECT

Think about a time or situation when your skills, patience, and/or wisdom was challenged. What did you learn about yourself through that experience?

Now think about a time when you were deeply scared but had to keep going. Maybe you had to give a presentation to a room full of people. Maybe someone cut you off in traffic and you had to engage in extreme maneuvering to stay safe. Maybe your child was in trouble and you couldn't help them. Where was God?

As the people were filled with expectation, and all were questioning in their hearts concerning John, whether he might be the Messiah, John answered all of them by saying, "I baptize you with water; but one who is more powerful than I is coming; I am not worthy to untie the thong of his sandals. He will baptize you with the Holy Spirit and fire. His winnowing fork is in his hand, to clear his threshing floor and to gather the wheat into his granary; but the chaff he will burn with unquenchable fire."

LUKE 3:15-17

TO HAVE INTEGRITY

I've been thinking a great deal about integrity. What does it mean to have integrity? What is lost when you compromise it?

Merriam-Webster defines integrity as the "state of being complete or undivided." When you hold your integrity, you are aligned, grounded in your sense of self as the clearest expression of what is true in you. Authenticity becomes the outward expression of your inner integrity. It's how the rest of us know that you are whole.

In the Gospel of Luke, we read a story of the early part of Jesus's ministry when John the Baptist was traveling the lands announcing the coming of the Messiah. I want to tell the story to you again but this time from a different translation called *The Message*. It has a wonderful way of helping us see the text:

"The interest of the people by now was building. They were all beginning to wonder, 'Could this John be the Messiah?' But John intervened: 'I'm baptizing you here in the river. The main character in this drama, to whom I'm a mere stagehand, will ignite the kingdom life, a fire, the Holy Spirit within you, changing you from the inside out. He's going to clean house—make a clean sweep of your lives. He'll place everything true in its proper place before God; everything false he'll put out with the trash to be burned.'"

John says, "I'm trying to live my best life, but Jesus is the real deal. He's the one we really need to follow." I respect that. Today, some people would say, "Look at me! Jesus is great, but I'm cool, too. If you agree, like my Facebook page!" But that wasn't the message John was given to proclaim. His was one of humility. Because he gave it without compromise, without ego, he did so with deep integrity.

One of the great gifts that Jesus brings to us is changing us "from the inside out." He calls to each of us to live aligned with our deepest wisdom and longings, to live integrated. When we fail to do this, we miss out on *real* living. We live a caricature of life, like what we see on reality TV, that gives the illusion of authenticity without the internal integrity forged from the fire of honest living.

One way to read this text is that Jesus comes to baptize us into our truest, most real selves. May it be so in my life and yours.

REFLECT

Write about a time when you felt yourself acting from a "state of being complete or undivided." How did you feel? What happened as a result?

We live in a "selfie" culture in which we are encouraged to present caricatures of our real lives on our social media spaces. We post only the pictures where we look good. We talk about our successes. What part of you gets hidden when you feel that you can't share what is true for you?

CLOSING PRAYER

Create in me
a clean heart, O God;
And put a new and
right spirit within me.
(*Psalm 51:10*)
Amen.

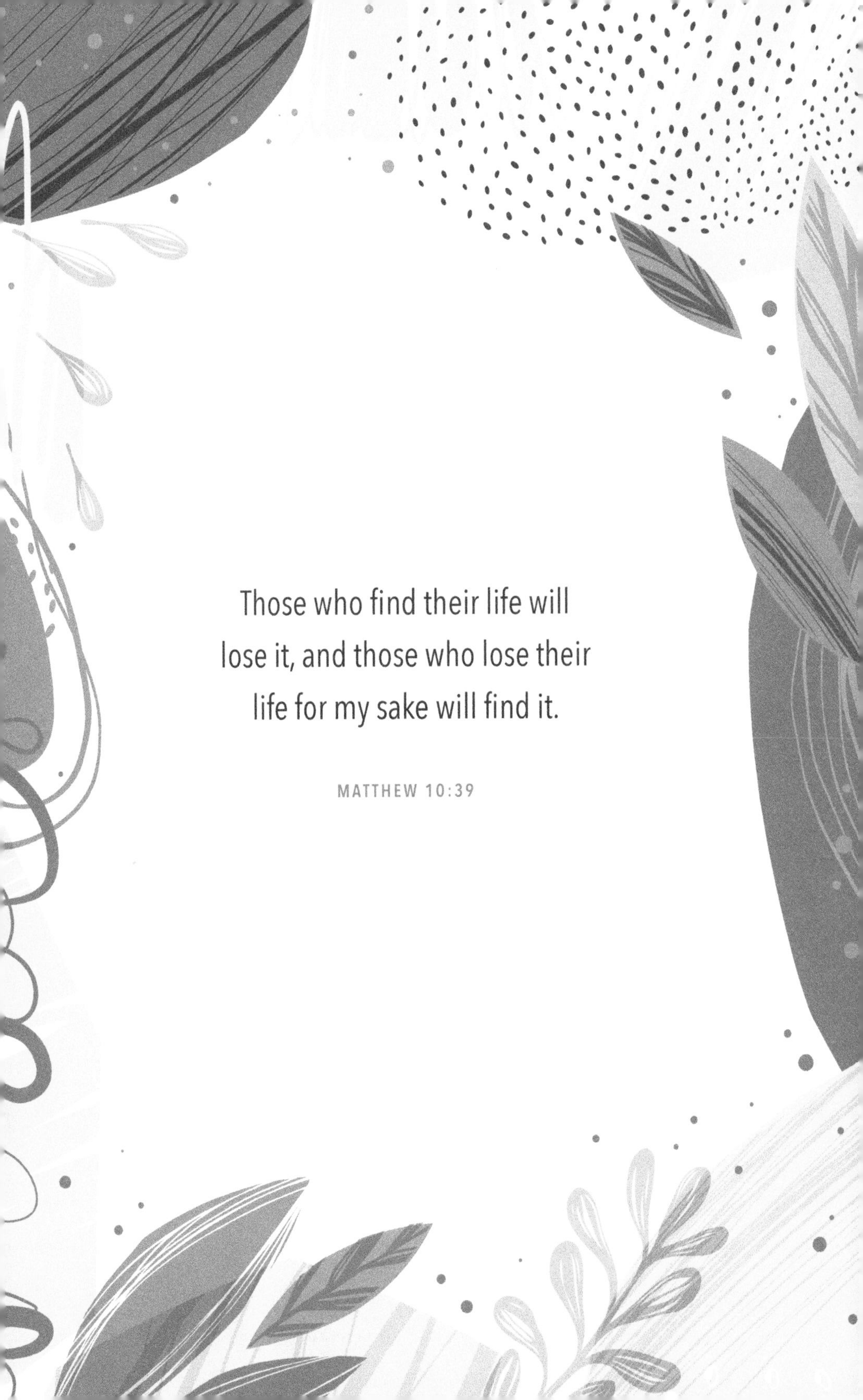

Those who find their life will lose it, and those who lose their life for my sake will find it.

MATTHEW 10:39

GETTING COMFORTABLE WITH BEING LOST

I have no sense of direction. That should probably alarm you since I am a pilot. Because of this, I get lost quite a bit unless I am using my GPS to guide me to my destination. I usually just end up on small detours, though occasionally I can find myself way off course.

I used to get anxious about these deviations and would carefully follow my GPS for the most direct route from point A to point B. But soon I found myself missing the adventure that comes with not being entirely sure of where you are going. I realized that I was more awake, more aware, and more curious about the journey when I wasn't certain I was on the proven path. I had the potential of flying a new route that no one else had traversed before. It's the subtle shift from being a follower to being an explorer—and it's the only path I know to a fulfilling life.

Author Martha Beck once said, "A good Wayfinder is someone who's comfortable losing the way."

Given all of the challenges we face as a community, especially with climate change, it seems we are being issued a new call to adventure. We must chart an original path forward to a sustainable future. We don't have any templates for getting us there—no one has figured this out yet—so it's up to us to get comfortable feeling lost while we find our way.

REFLECT

Think of a time when you felt utterly lost but not in real danger. You just didn't know where you were and had only a vague sense of where you were going. What did that experience invoke in you?

We also boast in our sufferings,
knowing that suffering produces
endurance, and endurance produces
character, and character produces
hope, and hope does not disappoint
us, because God's love has been
poured into our hearts through the
Holy Spirit that has been given to us.

ROMANS 5:3–5

THE GIFTS OF FAILURE

J. K. Rowling, the author of the Harry Potter series, gave a graduation speech at Harvard some years ago in which she talked about failure as one of the great gifts of life. She said:

"I have decided to talk to you about the benefits of failure. . . . Why? Simply because failure meant a stripping away of the inessential. I stopped pretending to myself that I was anything other than what I was, and I began to direct all of my energy into finishing the only work that mattered to me. Had I really succeeded at anything else, I might never have found the determination to succeed in the one arena where I believed I truly belonged. I was set free, because my greatest fear had been realized, and I was still alive, and I had a daughter whom I adored, and I had an old typewriter and a big idea. And so rock bottom became the solid foundation on which I rebuilt my life."

Could it be that failure is one of life's great teaching tools to make us stronger, more focused, and, in the end, braver? I don't wish failure on any of us. But we will fail, and we will get back up again, better for the journey.

The great hope for me in J. K. Rowling's speech is that hitting rock bottom was the start of her transformation. In the passage from Romans, Paul acknowledges the people's suffering but reminds them that while God is never the cause of suffering, God can use it for good. Struggle has a way of opening us, teaching us about endurance, character, and hope.

I pray that if failure comes your way, you will discover the strength of the foundation upon which your life is built. As the ancient words of Seneca remind us, *"As is a tale, so is life: not how long it is, but how good it is, is what matters."*

REFLECT

What lessons have you learned from failing?

The passage from Romans says that suffering produces endurance, character, and hope. Has that been true for you?

CLOSING PRAYER

Gracious God,
You know that I have failed in tasks that
I have undertaken. I have failed to do
that which was given for me to do and
which I wanted to do well. Let me learn
the lessons that strengthen me, but do
not let me fall into despair. I want to
rise again and try once more.
Amen.

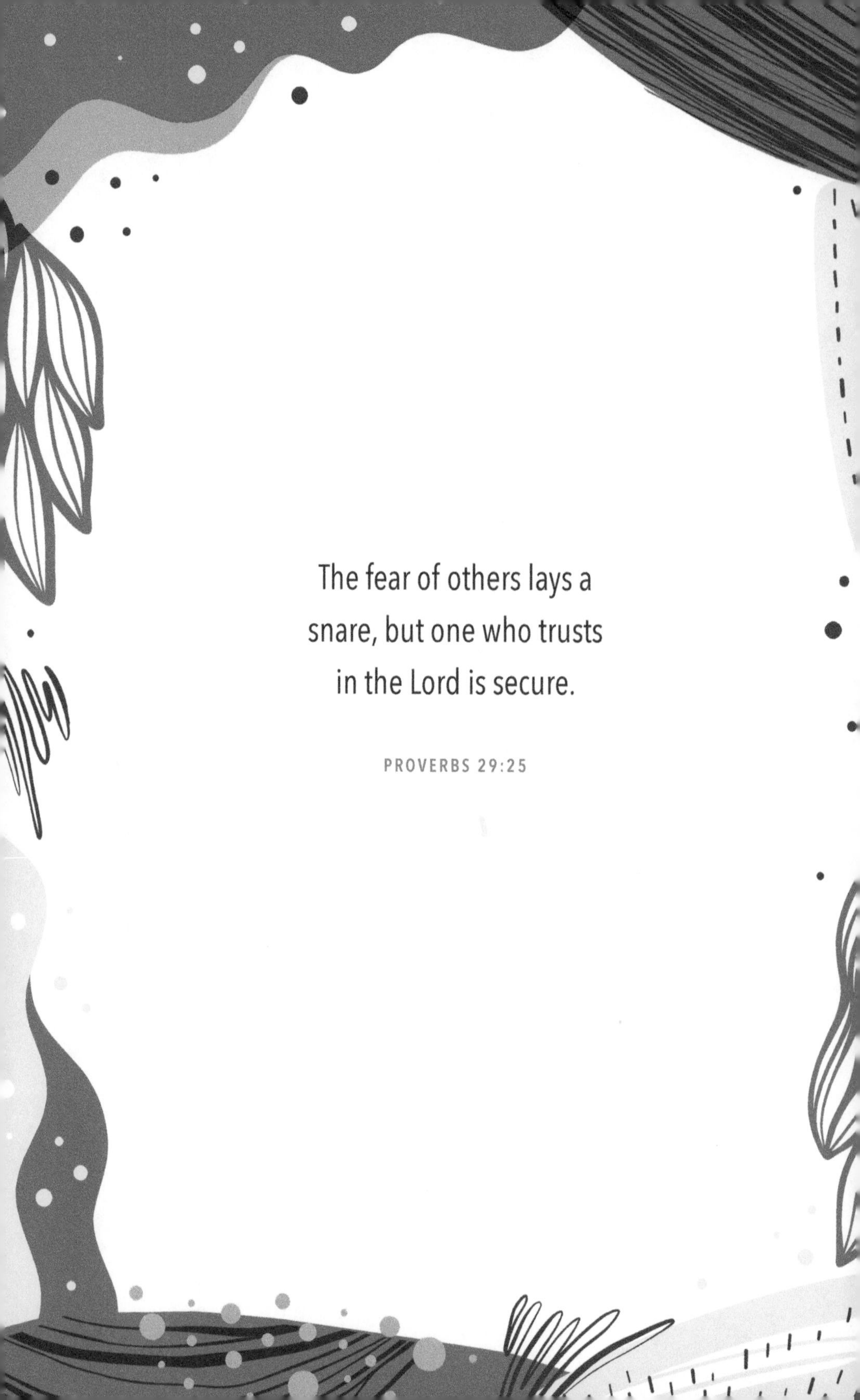

The fear of others lays a snare, but one who trusts in the Lord is secure.

PROVERBS 29:25

RISKING YOUR HAND FOR PEACE

Most of human history has been marked by people trying to figure out if they could trust one another. The great Shakespearean dramas all tell tales of trust given, trust violated, and finally trust redeemed. This theme certainly plays through to the world we live in today, where we wonder what countries we can trust, what neighbors we can trust, what news sources we can trust, what institutions we can trust, what leaders we can trust, and what ideas we can trust.

When we feel like we can't trust each other or our institutions, we become fearful, and we react in ways that close us off from one another, risking constant misunderstanding and raising the chance that we become hostile. It's a classic human drama. But it's not the way God would wish for us to be.

In St. Patrick's Cathedral in Dublin, Ireland, is an old door from 1492 with a rectangular hole cut in the middle. As the story goes, two feuding families, the Butlers of Ormonde and the FitzGeralds of Kildare, battled against one another. Sensing defeat on the battlefield, the Butler family retreated to the cathedral for safety. The FitzGeralds followed in pursuit, but instead of continuing the fighting, they proposed a truce. They promised the Butler family safe passage out of Dublin, but the Butlers refused, fearing it was a trap.

As a good faith gesture, George FitzGerald, the head of the FitzGerald family, ordered a hole to be cut into the door. He put his arm through it, offering peace. Convinced of his sincerity, the Butlers took his hand. The fighting stopped. This became the origin of the phrase *chance your arm.*

Imagine how our world would be different if we cut holes through the walls that separate us. What if our salvation, the way we break through the endless conflict and relentless fear, was by "chancing our arms" for one another? Of all that I know about God, I am certain of this: We are better, kinder, and more compassionate when we take the risk for peace.

REFLECT

Is there a person or situation in your life right now that needs you to take a "risk for peace"? What could you do today to extend your hand in reconciliation?

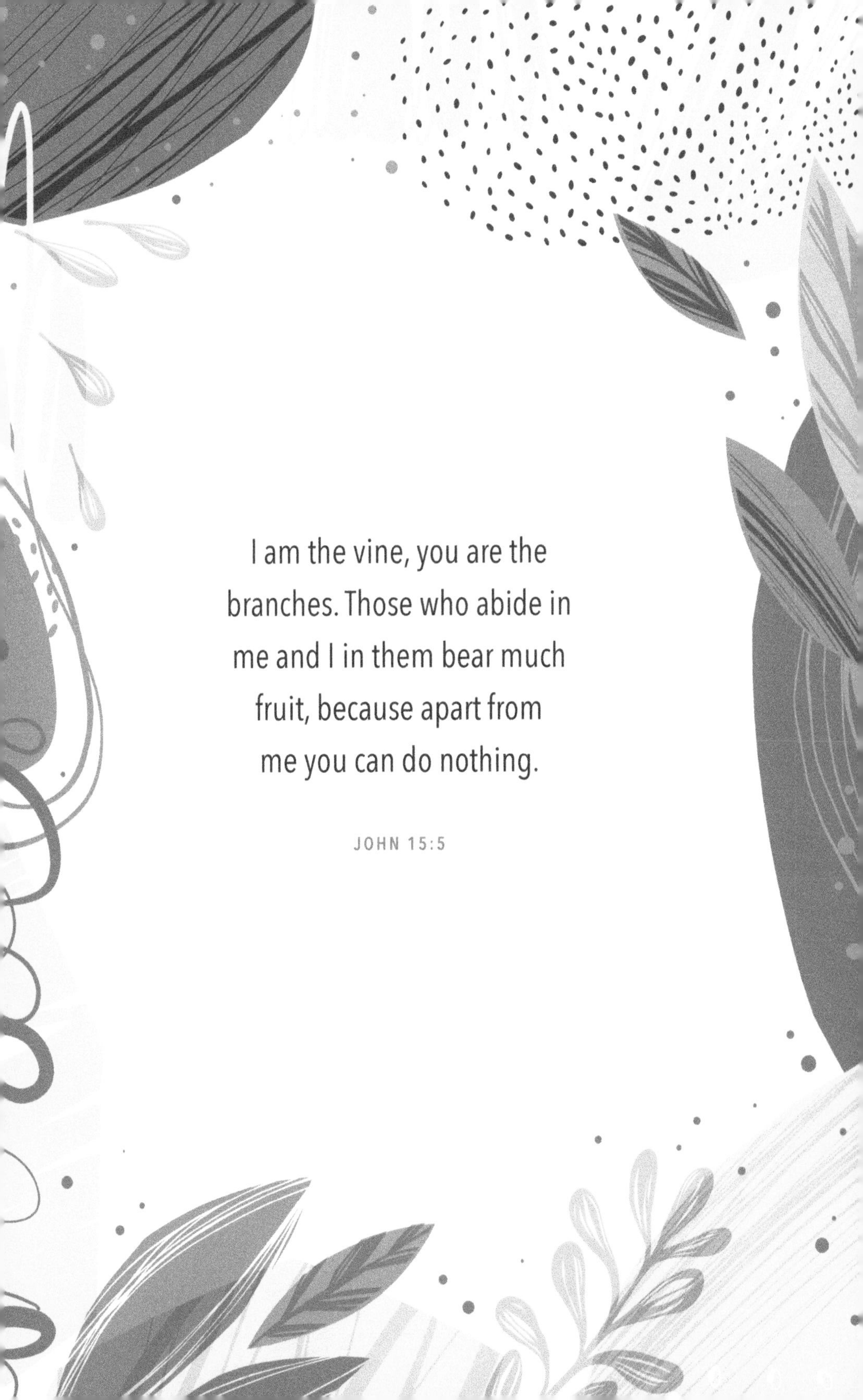

I am the vine, you are the branches. Those who abide in me and I in them bear much fruit, because apart from me you can do nothing.

JOHN 15:5

BLOOMING IN DARKNESS

I am lucky to have family that lives in the North Georgia mountains on land with a beautiful, wide creek that runs by their home. Beside the creek, they've created an incredible garden. They've been tending this garden for over 25 years, adding perennials, pulling weeds, planting vegetables, tilling the soil, repairing pathways, and plucking fresh-cut flowers that they put by our bedside when we come to visit. Each season brings a particular set of tasks, and the wise gardener senses the needs of the plants as the seasons change.

I was visiting them recently when they were in the pruning season. The flowers lay dormant, and the branches, once alive and full with blooms, needed trimming in order to grow fully in the coming season. Good gardeners know the different plants and what they need. They know what is vulnerable and needs extra care. They are patient and know that small things can become big with the right care.

People are the same. A friend, mentor, colleague, or parent is like a gifted gardener, loving each plant, knowing what is fragile, what is valuable, and what needs to be cut away. People grow and bloom with you when this is the case. You help each other sow the seeds of new possibility and grow strong supports to lean against when needed.

The Gospel writer John talked about Jesus using many metaphors of vines and branches. He talked about pruning and bearing fruit as a way of recognizing that the spiritual life is one of letting go of anything holding us back. Then we are freed to generate what will carry us forward. It's the cycle of life as God designed it: life, death, life again.

I pray that you prune away anything that is holding you back so that you might bloom magnificently in the coming spring.

REFLECT

Who in your life has been a "green thumb" friend, helping you grow into who you are today?

What in yourself or in your life could be trimmed away to make room for new growth?

CLOSING PRAYER

May we travel through this day as
if walking through a beautiful garden,
embraced by the flowers, trees,
and vines of those who see in us
the seeds of love.
Amen.

What does it profit them if they gain the whole world, but lose or forfeit themselves?

LUKE 9:25

FIX EVERYTHING, CHANGE NOTHING

You may have heard the story of a man who came across three masons who were working at chipping chunks of granite from large blocks. The first seemed unhappy at his job, chipping away and frequently looking at his watch. When the man asked what he was doing, the first mason responded rather curtly, "I'm hammering this stupid rock, and I can't wait 'til five when I can go home."

A second mason, seemingly more interested in his work, was hammering diligently. When asked what he was doing, he answered, "Well, I'm molding this block of rock so that it can be used with others to construct a wall. It's not bad work, but I'll sure be glad when it's done."

A third mason was hammering at his block fervently, taking time to stand back and admire his work. He chipped off small pieces until he was satisfied that it was the best he could do. When he was questioned about his work, he stopped, gazed skyward, and proudly proclaimed, "I am building a cathedral."

The bigger your vision, the more magnificent your life could be. Most of us want to fix everything but change nothing. We want to be fit and strong but still eat anything we want and not have to endure tough workouts. We want to build great cathedrals, but we don't want to work with the architects, buy the supplies, or carry the massive stones. Our vision may be grand, but our application is half-hearted, fearful, and impotent.

Becoming something or someone exceptional is not an accidental undertaking. No one accidentally builds a magnificent cathedral. We intentionally decide to do these things and then undertake the preparing, planning, and training to make them a reality.

How are you spending your life today? Are you angrily chipping at rocks? Are you molding rocks, waiting for the day to end? Or are you building a cathedral? Your answer will tell the world how great you wish to be.

REFLECT

We don't all need to build great cathedrals. Some of us will build great friendships. Some will build great companies. Some will build great families. What matters is that you know what you are building. So . . . what are you building?

For everything there is a season,
and a time for every matter
under heaven: a time to be
born, and a time to die. . . .

ECCLESIASTES 3:1–2

FOR EVERYTHING THERE IS A SEASON

In today's chaotic world, I wonder about the long-term use of our obsession with youth, immortality, and progress. It seems like we are running from progress rather than to progress—we are missing gifts in one another right before our eyes.

A parable tells of a man who used to carry water every day to his village, using two large pitchers tied on either end of a piece of wood, which he placed across his shoulders. One of the pitchers was older than the other and was full of small cracks. Every time the man came back along the path to his house, half of the water was lost.

For two years, the man made the same journey. The younger pitcher was always very proud of the way it did its work and was sure that it was up to the task for which it had been created. The other pitcher was mortally ashamed that it could carry out only half of its task, even though it knew that the cracks were the result of long years of work.

So ashamed was the older pitcher that one day, when the man was preparing to fill it up with water from the well, it decided to speak to him.

"I wish to apologize because, due to my age, you manage to take home only half the water you fill me with, and thus quench only half the thirst awaiting you in your house."

The man smiled and said, "When we go back, be sure to take a careful look at the path."

The pitcher did as the man asked and noticed many flowers and plants growing along one side of the path.

"Do you see how much more beautiful nature is on your side of the road?" the man remarked. "I knew you had cracks, but I decided to take advantage of them. I sowed vegetables and flowers there, and you always watered them. I've picked dozens of roses to decorate my house, and my children have lettuce, cabbage, and onions to eat. If you were not the way you are, I could never have done this. We all, at some point, grow old and acquire other qualities, and these can always be turned to good advantage."

Ecclesiastes 3:1–8 reminds us that for everything there is a season and a time for every matter under heaven. All of it—every moment—is a wonderful, God-gifted journey.

REFLECT

What can the cracks in your well-lived, worked-out life teach you today? Try looking for the flowers to show you the way.

CLOSING PRAYER

May the cycle of your life
help you come of age
as you learn that each pass
brings out something new
within you all along
but made visible only
from the cracks you gain
along the way.
Amen.

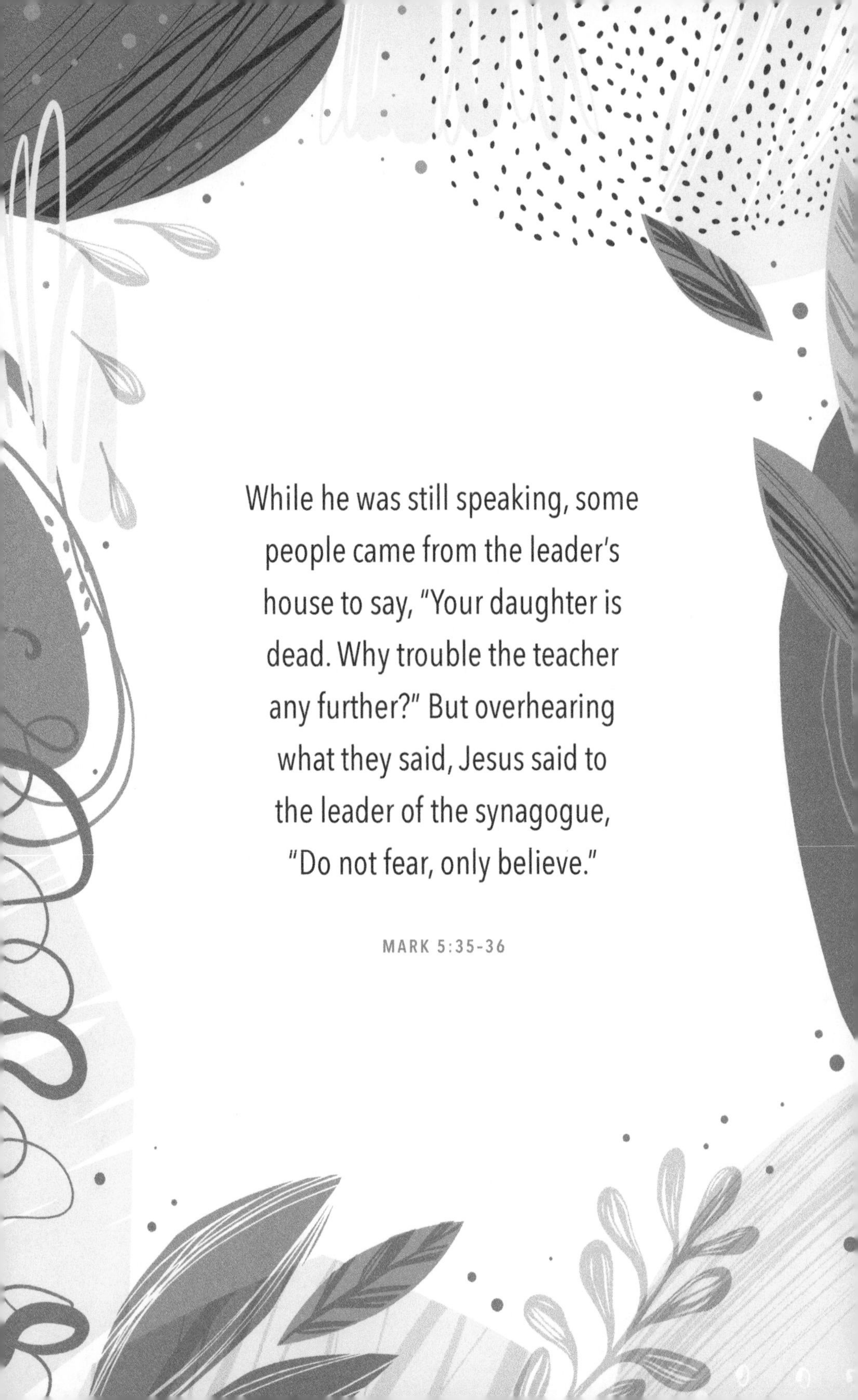

While he was still speaking, some people came from the leader's house to say, "Your daughter is dead. Why trouble the teacher any further?" But overhearing what they said, Jesus said to the leader of the synagogue, "Do not fear, only believe."

MARK 5:35-36

DO NOT FEAR, ONLY BELIEVE

Lately, people have been sharing stories from their lives that have made a profound impact on me. Each of these stories has twists and turns that no one saw coming. Sue's husband was diagnosed with cancer and died within three months. Andy unexpectedly lost his job. Camille's brother was killed in a drive-by shooting.

We all go through trying times, when our faith is tested. Imagine being the mother who was told that her daughter had died in this passage from Mark. It's the worst news any parent could receive.

Some years ago, I was called to come to the hospital late one night. The nurse who called said that a family was there who needed support. I was on call that evening, so it was both my responsibility and my honor to come.

When I got to the hospital, I learned that a mother and father were in the patient care room. Their 16-year-old daughter had been in a devastating car accident that night and had died from the trauma. The hospital staff were waiting for me to arrive before telling the family.

The doctor and I walked into the room together and introduced ourselves. In that moment, my experience of time slowed. I knew that with a few brief words from the doctor, these parents' lives would be forever changed. I wished with all of me that we could NOT speak the words, that they would not be true. I wished we could save them from the pain that was to come. But telling the truth is often the hardest and bravest gift we give to one another.

The doctor said, "I'm sorry. Your daughter didn't survive her injuries from the accident." And then we all wept. The pain was terrible. The loss was palpable.

The mother turned to me, anger flashing in her eyes. "How could God allow this? What kind of God would take my little girl?"

"No God that I believe in would ever take your little girl," I said. "God is just as heartbroken as you are right now. Your daughter was in an accident. God didn't cause that accident. God grieves that such accidents happen and is here with you in the pain."

They were inadequate words for the moment, but I do believe them to be true. God is never the source of our pain and does not randomly take one life and spare another. While that is popular theology, it isn't good theology. The truth is that God is with us in the twists and turns of life, showing up in the kindness of strangers, the care of nurses, the compassion of first responders, the love of friends who come in our moments of deep need. God works through those of us who show love, compassion, and kindness.

It's that show of love that allows us to move toward healing. That family will never "get over" the loss of their daughter. They still miss her every day and wish that the accident had never happened. But they have also claimed a future for themselves that celebrates the time they had with their daughter while they encourage other families to cherish the time they have with one another. By telling their story to others, they find healing for themselves.

In this passage, Jesus is inviting us to remember that even in the most trying times of life, God is with us. We are never abandoned. God brings resurrection from the crucifying experiences of life. God never wishes us pain, but when it comes, he works for our healing and wholeness.

REFLECT

Think of a difficult situation in your life, past or present. What questions do you want to ask God about that situation? How do you believe God is present for you?

As you consider the same situation, where can you see or feel others offering love, kindness, and compassion?

You will know the
truth, and the truth
will make you free.

JOHN 8:32

DONE AND FREE

I was looking for investors for my latest project. But I wasn't asking people to simply give me money—I wanted to invite them to invest their time and expertise. Each conversation is different and teaches me something about fear, generosity, kindness, and collaboration.

In one such case, I walked into a potential investor's plush office, looking out over Bryant Park in Manhattan. He didn't stand to greet me as I sat down in the chair in front of his desk.

"What are you trying to accomplish?" he asked me, staring down at me over the rims of his glasses.

One more time, I calmly explained what I was working to create. I wasn't asking permission. I was asking him to join in.

"Tell me, what is in this for me?" he said. I suggested that he could ask a different question, a better one. Try: What is in it for us? The "collective" us. The "common good" us. The "we are all in it together" us.

"Well, it's a nice dream. You won't succeed. Not without my help. And I am afraid I can't give it to you," he said as he leaned back in his chair, folding his arms across his chest with a smirk on his face.

I nodded, stood, and walked out almost giddy to be free of him. Good things usually come when people underestimate me. More than that, good things come when they underestimate all of us as we work together for the common good. Trust is the currency of change.

Then it hit me: He had taught me a valuable lesson by accident. We are free when we are authentic. We are powerful when we are collaborative. We are unstoppable when we are generous. Jesus was trying to teach this to his disciples in this text from John. He was saying, "Live a generous life with genuine integrity, one like I am modeling for you, and you will find the freedom you seek."

REFLECT

Can you remember a time when someone turned you down and it was the best thing that could have happened to you? What did that experience teach you?

Why do you think Jesus connected truth and freedom?

CLOSING PRAYER

God,
Let all that confines me fall away.
Let all that holds me back be removed.
Let all that leads me astray be rejected.
Let everything in me that longs for truth
be the path I follow to freedom in you.
Amen.

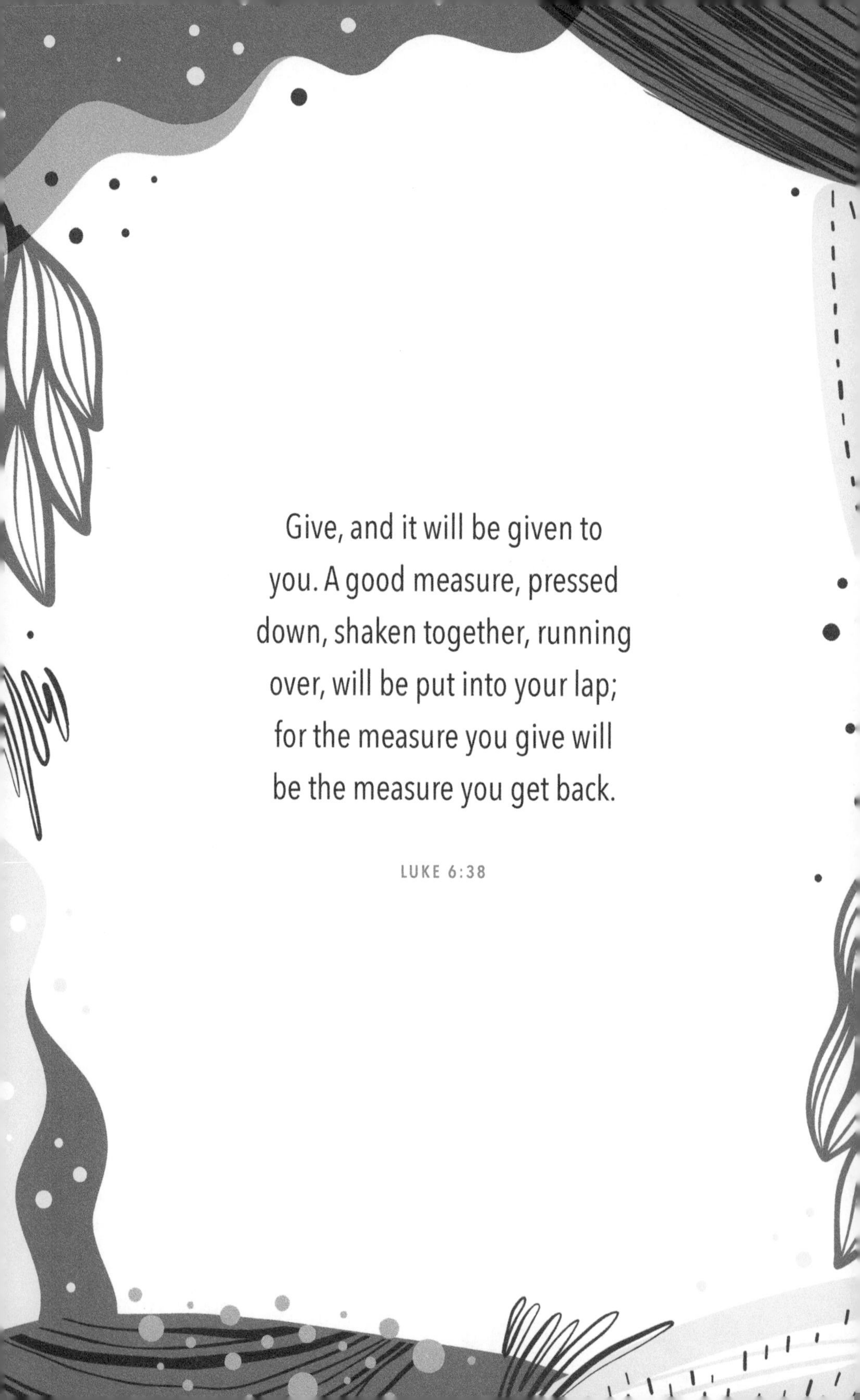

Give, and it will be given to you. A good measure, pressed down, shaken together, running over, will be put into your lap; for the measure you give will be the measure you get back.

LUKE 6:38

BEING GENEROUS

Jesus talked about money more than any other topic in all of his ministry. He understood that we all struggle to believe that we have enough. We get scared that we will be left out, so we hoard our gifts, possessions, and resources out of fear instead of offering them to one another out of a sense of abundance. Abundance, Jesus says, is the currency of God. You can't know God and not be a generous person.

Recently I attended a fundraising event for The Link Counseling Center in Atlanta. It is an extraordinary center providing affordable counseling services to thousands of people in the region since 1971. I have benefited from—and been inspired by—their work for years.

I participated in their "Miracle Ball" because I am a philanthropist. By that, I mean I "seek to promote the welfare of others, especially by the donation of money to good causes." That is how Merriam-Webster defines philanthropy. I bet if you considered why you support organizations with your gifts, you would say the same.

I have come to understand philanthropy through a wider lens. Giving even at the smallest levels has brought me such fulfillment. I now look for others to connect to good causes and encourage them to give as well.

I see it as part of my calling as a generous person to invite others in my life to give generously too. I take them with me to fundraisers. I tell them about organizations I support doing critical work to make the world more just and generous. I celebrate when they offer gifts because I see that as an investment in our common good.

I am finally coming to understand that this is why Jesus talked about money so much—more than any other topic. He knew that being generous was the only way to free ourselves from the desperate grip of fear. When we are generous, we trust that we will have enough. More than that, we finally learn that we *are* enough and always have been. I believe the way the world works, the way God designed this world to work, is that God—through *you*—can take the smallest of gifts and multiply them in the most extraordinary ways so that they become the abundance of the community. That is the most precious gift of all.

REFLECT

How would you describe generosity in your life?

What have you learned about yourself by being a generous woman?

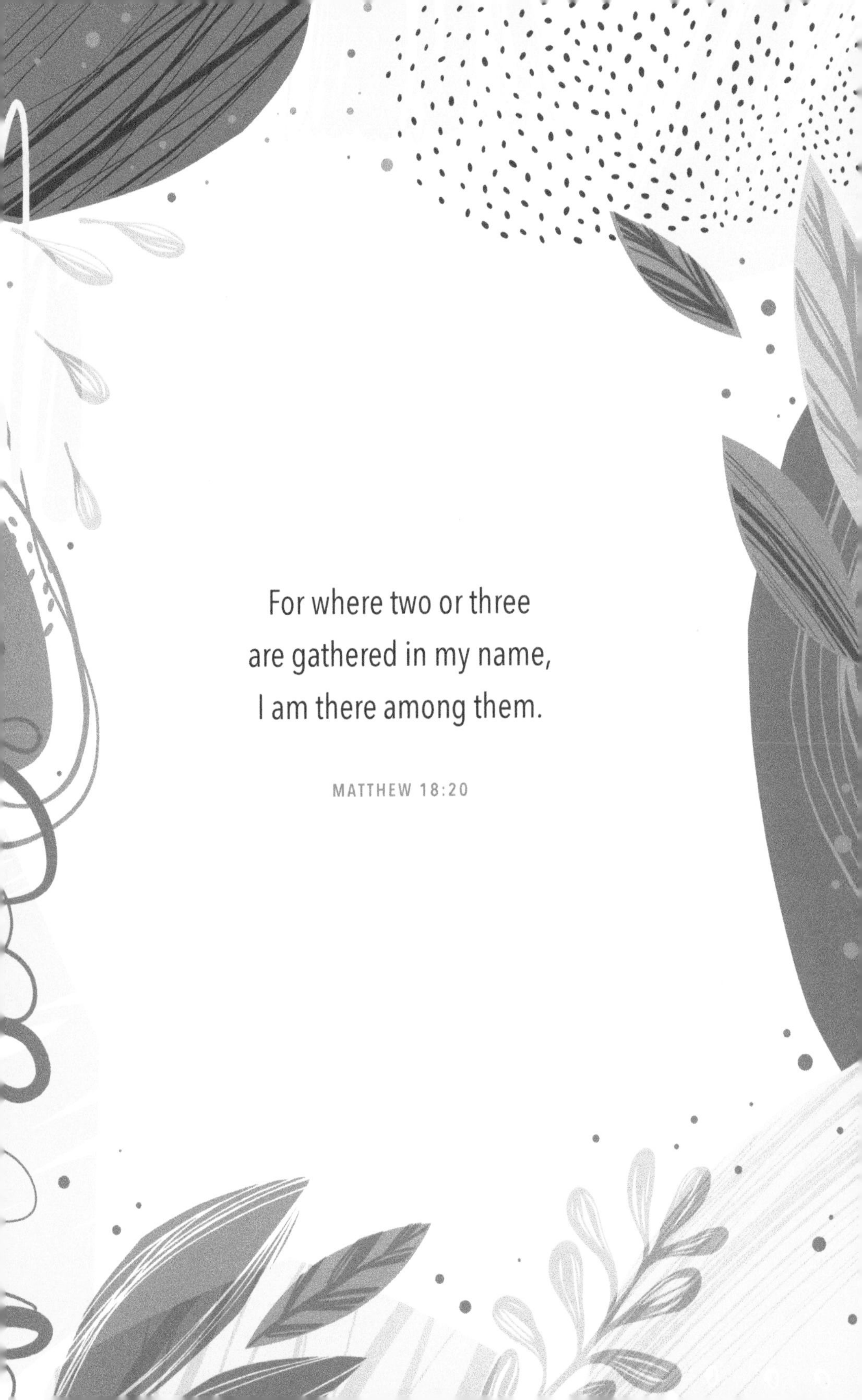

For where two or three
are gathered in my name,
I am there among them.

MATTHEW 18:20

THE GIFT OF LISTENING

I love this biblical passage. It describes for me the holiness of moments of real listening. The health, wholeness, and holiness of a new relationship forming. I once saw a card that said, "You can't hate someone whose story you know." You don't have to like the story or even the person telling you their story. But listening creates a relationship. We move closer to one another.

Margaret Wheatley is a writer, speaker, teacher, and sociologist who has worked across the globe with governments, corporations, non-profits, and universities studying organizational change and how we create healthy communities. In other words, she looks at the way the world works best and helps the rest of us see what is sitting in front of our eyes.

In her book *A Simpler Way*, she tells of a beautiful encounter between a teacher and student. This teacher had a 16-year-old in her class who was disruptive. He would shout at the teacher and other students. But instead of calling the principal in for disciplinary action, she simply sat down next to him. He got up and paced, and it took him a while to settle. Eventually, he sat close to her, and she began asking him questions about his life. He talked to her, telling her stories that he hadn't told anyone in a long time. She didn't give advice or try to "fix" him. She didn't need to because he was working out his life as he talked. He needed to be heard, so she offered him a simple gift: She listened.

Every one of us needs to be heard. Our stories, birthed from deep within us, reveal truths that we long to bring into the world. Our stories hold our vulnerabilities. They communicate our pain. They share our joy. They create portals for others to see into us. We need to tell our stories to one another, and we need to listen to others tell theirs. It's in the meeting of your story with mine that we find our common humanity. That is when we finally see that we are all God's children and God is with us.

REFLECT

Write about a time when you shared a story about yourself and you had the sense that the person listening could hear beyond your words to see deep, true parts of you. Then write about a time when you listened to someone else with such openness and gained such vision.

What story is true about your life that you are too afraid to speak about?

CLOSING PRAYER

May you discern
What stories to tell
What stories to receive
What stories to live.
Amen.

Then the Lord said, "I have observed the misery of my people who are in Egypt; I have heard their cry on account of their taskmasters. . . . So come, I will send you to Pharaoh to bring my people, the Israelites, out of Egypt." But Moses said to God, "Who am I that I should go to Pharaoh, and bring the Israelites out of Egypt?"

EXODUS 3:7, 10–11

I FEEL LIKE AN IMPOSTER

Moses was one of the great leaders of ancient Israel. But he didn't think he was. He is our first example of "imposter syndrome" in the Bible. He's a shepherd, out wandering in the wilderness taking care of his sheep. Then God appears to him in the form of a burning bush and says, "Moses, I need you to go rescue my people from slavery." Moses says, "Um, who am I to do that? I don't speak well. People won't believe me. I'm the worst choice." But God says, "Go!" So he goes, with fear and trepidation, because he is certain he will fail. Turns out he doesn't. That's good news for the rest of us.

Recently I had breakfast with an Atlanta pastor who has been a friend of mine for 15 years. I adore her. We just "get" each other. She is the pastor of a large church in Atlanta, a brilliant preacher, energetic leader, and all-round great human. Anyone who meets her thinks she is amazing—because she is.

Those same people would be shocked to know we spent the morning talking about imposter syndrome—about feeling like we never measure up. Even after all of this time and all we have accomplished, it isn't quite enough.

Of course, that's nonsense. But it's still real.

All of us experience moments of insecurity when we wonder about the difference we make and fear the judgment of others. That helps because it means we can remind each other that we don't need to prove our value. Our value is given. All we need to do is support each other in awakening and celebrate our becoming.

Carry on, all of you fierce Wisdom Warriors. You are making a difference.

REFLECT

Reflect on a time when you had a major case of imposter syndrome. What happened? What did you learn?

When have you felt God call you to do something and you felt completely unprepared or unqualified to do it?

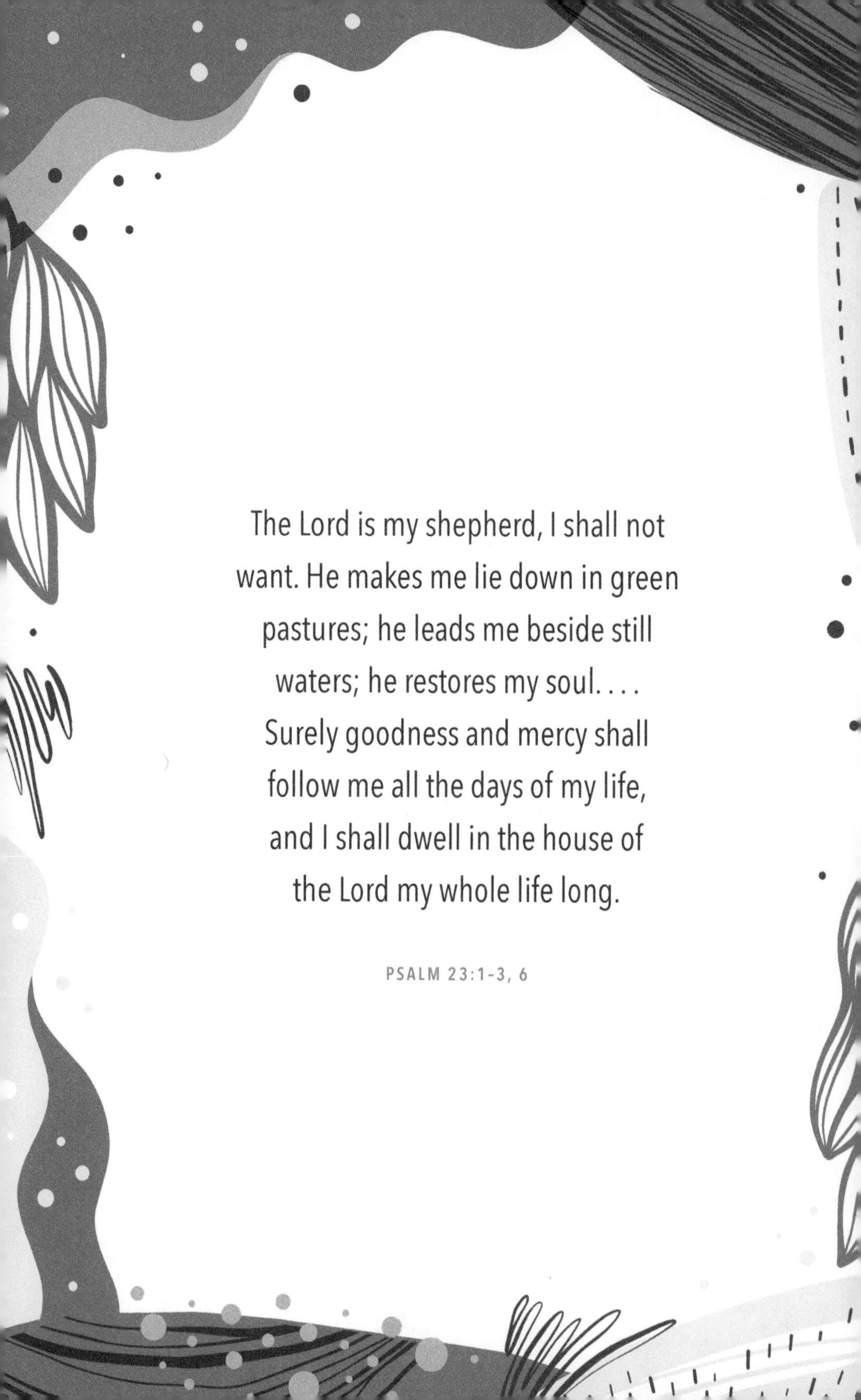

The Lord is my shepherd, I shall not want. He makes me lie down in green pastures; he leads me beside still waters; he restores my soul. . . . Surely goodness and mercy shall follow me all the days of my life, and I shall dwell in the house of the Lord my whole life long.

PSALM 23:1–3, 6

WHAT VERSES SUSTAIN YOU?

When I was in my second year of seminary, I was assigned to serve as a chaplain in a care facility for people suffering from Alzheimer's disease. The floor was absolute chaos most of the time. Ms. Betty would regularly take off her clothes and walk naked through the halls. Mr. Samuel would go to the nursing station thinking he was checking into a hotel. He would hand them a piece of paper and ask for his room. Mrs. Margaret would carry around a small baby doll believing that she was its mom.

My job on the floor was to lead them in a daily worship experience. At first, I had no idea where to start. With everyone living in their own fantasy lands, how could I create anything that could bring them together?

Fortunately, a wiser clergywoman was also working on that floor with me. I will never forget that first day, when I was totally overwhelmed and didn't know what to do with the chaos that surrounded me. She simply stood in the middle of the common room and started reciting Psalm 23. By the end of the first line, every patient in the room was saying it with her, their eyes locked on her face while the poetry of the psalm poured from their mouths.

She led them in reciting the psalm three times. By the end of the third time, you could feel a palpable calm in everyone in the room. We were comforted and at peace.

Psalm 23 is one of the wonderful passages that has provided comfort to people for generations. It was originally penned by King David as he faced the threat of war and the possibility that he could at any moment be killed. He talks about his faith in God as the source of his comfort. God's spirit guides him beside still waters and restores his soul. God guides him on the right paths even if they lead him into the darkest of valleys. Because King David trusts God, he does not fear evil. So even as he faces the presence of his enemies, he feels God anointing him, and his sense of gratitude overflows.

This psalm is a beautiful poem that captures our greatest hope that in the face of suffering, we will be comforted. Given how many of us have committed this psalm to memory, it seems we all need to hear its message at some point in life.

Some texts speak so purely to our experiences of pain and hope that they get woven into the deepest parts of us. In the end, when we know little else, they remain keys to peace for our restless and weary souls.

REFLECT

What texts have become woven into the fabric of your being? How do they bring you calm and peace?

CLOSING PRAYER

May the wisdom of our elders be
written upon our hearts,
May the presence of the saints
be woven into our being,
May the peace of Christ be
with us always,
For all the days of our lives.
Amen.

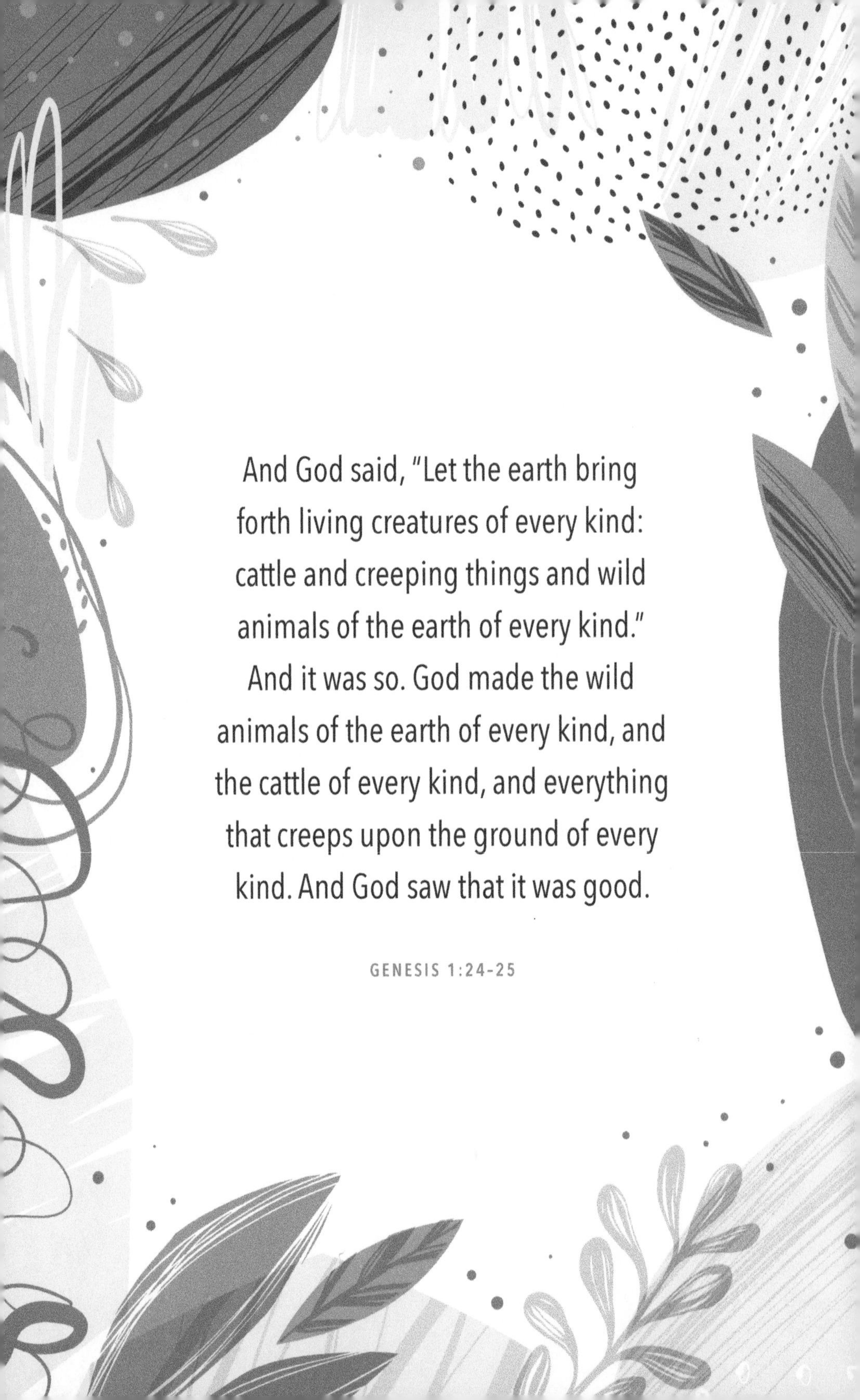

And God said, "Let the earth bring forth living creatures of every kind: cattle and creeping things and wild animals of the earth of every kind." And it was so. God made the wild animals of the earth of every kind, and the cattle of every kind, and everything that creeps upon the ground of every kind. And God saw that it was good.

GENESIS 1:24-25

WHAT MATTERS IN THE END

Recently, we had to say goodbye to our 16-year-old golden retriever, Abby. If you are an animal person, you know the pain of losing a pet who has been an intimate part of your life for so many years. Abby was a beautiful combination of endless unconditional love and quirky childlike playfulness. She liked to eat rocks, have her back end scratched, drink from nasty mud puddles, and roll in dirt patches. And then, of course, she wanted to snuggle.

As she passed peacefully in our home, I remembered the words of Jack Kornfield, who said, "In the end, just three things matter: how well we have lived, how well we have loved, and how well we have learned to let go." Abby nailed all three.

Women often have a close connection to animals and the earth. In the Genesis story, we were created from the same ground from which God created the animals that walk the earth. We come from the same soil. We were designed by God to be kin and partners to one another, living together in peace. Abby taught me that lesson.

Today our house feels empty, but I am left with the deepest sense of gratitude for having been loved by such a magnificent animal. She made me a better person and taught me about life and love. I suppose that is the final great lesson animals teach us—they show us how to love with abandon so that we might do the same for another person.

REFLECT

What would you tell a child about your life as a journey of living, loving, and letting go?

If you have pets, what life lessons have they taught you?

Peter answered him, "Lord, if it is you, command me to come to you on the water." He said, "Come." So Peter got out of the boat, started walking on the water, and came toward Jesus.

MATTHEW 14:28-29

HOW DID I GET HERE?

Do you ever wonder, “How did I get here?” I can imagine that is what Peter was thinking when he, likely in a fit of reckless enthusiasm, asked if he could try walking on water. He had just seen Jesus walking on the water in the midst of a storm. What better way to show his faith than to try as well? After all, Jesus was always telling people to “follow” him. Peter wanted to be first in line!

He wanted to be first, until he came to his senses and saw the waves. He felt the rain beating against him. He felt the water rising up his legs. Then, in fear, he cried out for Jesus to save him. I can imagine Peter getting back into the boat and thinking, “How did I get here, and what was I thinking?”

Many of us have powerful encounters with people or opportunities that set our life onto a path we could not have predicted. We find ourselves thinking, “How did I get here?” Sometimes we get “here” because our partner got a job in a new city or our kids took on hobbies we would never have chosen for ourselves. Sometimes “here” happens because our company moves its headquarters. Sometimes “here” is because we wake up one day and decide to make life changes more aligned with who we are as opposed to who others want us to be.

Most of us are grateful for our lives and all that we have gained along the way. Questioning how we got here isn’t out of dissatisfaction. It’s a curiosity that can teach us something of who we are and who we might become.

Is this where you intended to be or where you just ended up by default? Did you shape your life, or did life shape you? Need or want to change anything going forward?

I admire Peter for wanting to walk on water, even if he failed to make it all the way. At least he tried. Eleven of the other disciples didn’t. Peter, of all of the disciples, wanted to be in the present moment with Jesus. He wanted to be “here” even with all of the twists and turns that such an adventure would bring. I hope I am that brave.

You don't have to walk on water to live a purposeful and faithful life. The important lesson is making sure that you are choosing "here" consciously. As my coach taught me many years ago, everyone gets somewhere in life. The rare person gets somewhere on purpose.

REFLECT

How did you get "here" in your life? Think back over all of the people, chance opportunities, risks, and adventures that led you to this place.

Would you change anything about your "here" to help you connect more fully to yourself and God?

CLOSING PRAYER

Lord God,
I pray this day that I will not hide from your invitations to follow you, for fear of hurting others' feelings or giving up too much. I know that whatever path you lead me down, it will be most true for both me and you.
Amen.

"Go, gather all the Jews to be found in Susa, and hold a fast on my behalf, and neither eat nor drink for three days, night or day. I and my maids will also fast as you do. After that I will go to the king, though it is against the law; and if I perish, I perish."

ESTHER 4:16

PLAYING TO WIN OR TRYING NOT TO LOSE

Trying not to lose is different from playing to win. Trying not to lose ties you to scarcity. You adopt a low tolerance for risk. Your willingness to imagine, innovate, pivot, and dare to create something new is nonexistent. You are trying not to lose what you have, so you hold on tight and don't make any sudden moves.

Playing to win is the opposite energy. If you want to play to win in your company, you hire people smarter than you. You create an environment that rewards creativity. You articulate a vision that both inspires and propels your organization forward.

Playing to win as a Christian woman means you invest in your community and your family while also investing in yourself. You feed the hungry, nurture your family, house the homeless, cherish your partner, care for the sick, and work for the collective common good. You also pray/meditate, take care of your body, learn from our sacred texts, and listen to your "still small voice" within.

A lot of women struggle with playing to win. We sometimes think we don't deserve to succeed. We feel we need to prove our worth. That is when it matters that we remember Queen Esther. When faced with the knowledge that her husband was allowing the murder of her people, she had to make a decision. Was she going to stay quiet and stay safe? Or was she going to act to save them?

Her uncle, Mordecai, made her choice clear. She worried that if she called attention to herself, she would be called out as a Jew. She had the option to hide. But Mordecai reminded her that she was queen for just such a moment as this. "Play to win," he said, because there was too much to lose.

She did. Queen Esther was fierce and focused and saved her people through her bravery. Hers is a wonderful story of a woman facing her fear and playing to win. The final revelation is that we all have her courage in us. We follow in her footsteps.

Playing to win simply means that you believe your best days are ahead. Trying not to lose means your best days are over.

You choose.

REFLECT

What do you think about the difference between playing to win and trying not to lose? Do those competing ideas resonate with you?

In what areas of your life are you trying not to lose?

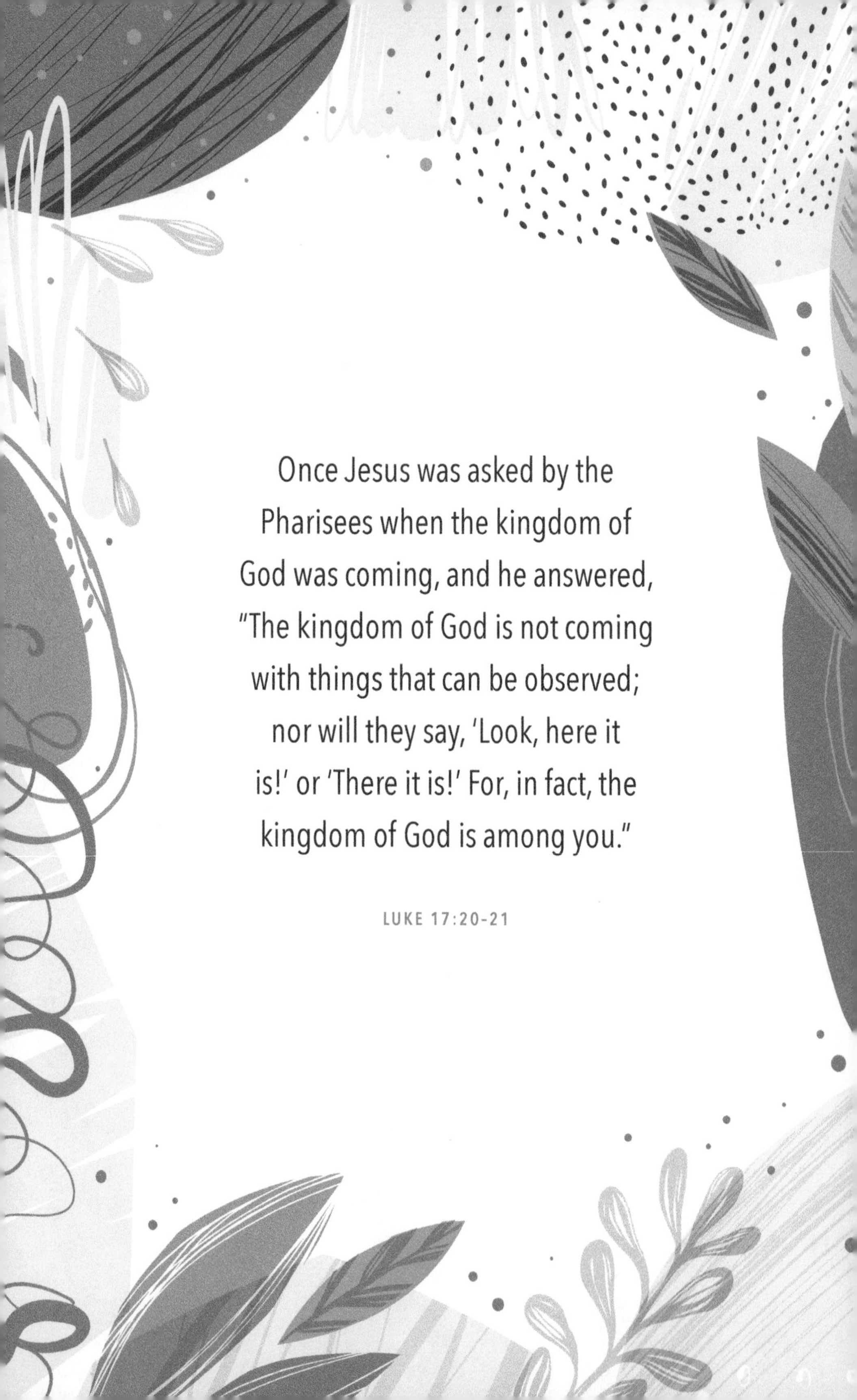

Once Jesus was asked by the Pharisees when the kingdom of God was coming, and he answered, "The kingdom of God is not coming with things that can be observed; nor will they say, 'Look, here it is!' or 'There it is!' For, in fact, the kingdom of God is among you."

LUKE 17:20-21

WHAT WE VALUE

As a culture, we have moved from valuing wisdom to seeking knowledge to chasing information. We are now overwhelmed by information without the wisdom to know how to use it.

Many years ago, ancient Polynesian sailors could travel hundreds of miles in their wooden canoes without navigational equipment and never lose their way. They used wayfinding techniques and knowledge passed by oral tradition from master to apprentice, often in the form of song. They developed the ability to read the currents, the stars, the winds, the flight of birds, and the clouds. They approached the open ocean with respect. They, in time, developed intuitions that served as a guide for them as they traversed the oceans and opened new lands to discovery.

Today we face the challenge of learning to traverse the vast ocean of the digital age. It's tempting to think that more data, faster machines, better algorithms, and artificial intelligence will create a better world and make us wiser humans. But more and more of us are sensing that those tools, while interesting for what they can offer us, are insufficient for the journey we must now undertake as a global society. We are forever lost if we rely only on our information. Our technology will not save us or carry us to a promised paradise. We must develop our intuition, ancient and dormant within us, to guide us to a sustainable future.

The journey of a woman or man is one marked by the deepening of our sense of self and maturing of our internal wisdom. As we age, we tap into an internal source of wisdom that has been with us all along, but time reveals its true power. If we are lucky, we learn the lessons from generations that have gone before us so that we make new mistakes, learn new lessons, and teach the next generation of young ones. Becoming a wise human takes time. It's a slow technology but more valuable than all the information and knowledge in the world.

Jesus tried to teach us about this journey of becoming fully human, as we see in Luke 17:20–21. Look inside, he says. The way is already within you. You need only slow down enough to intuit it.

REFLECT

What have you noticed about yourself when you are moving too fast? What about when you slow down?

How do you know when you are navigating your life by intuition? What do you see, sense, and know?

CLOSING PRAYER

May the wise women
who lived before us
meet us in the waves of change,
teaching us to navigate
by the winds of our internal knowing.
Amen.

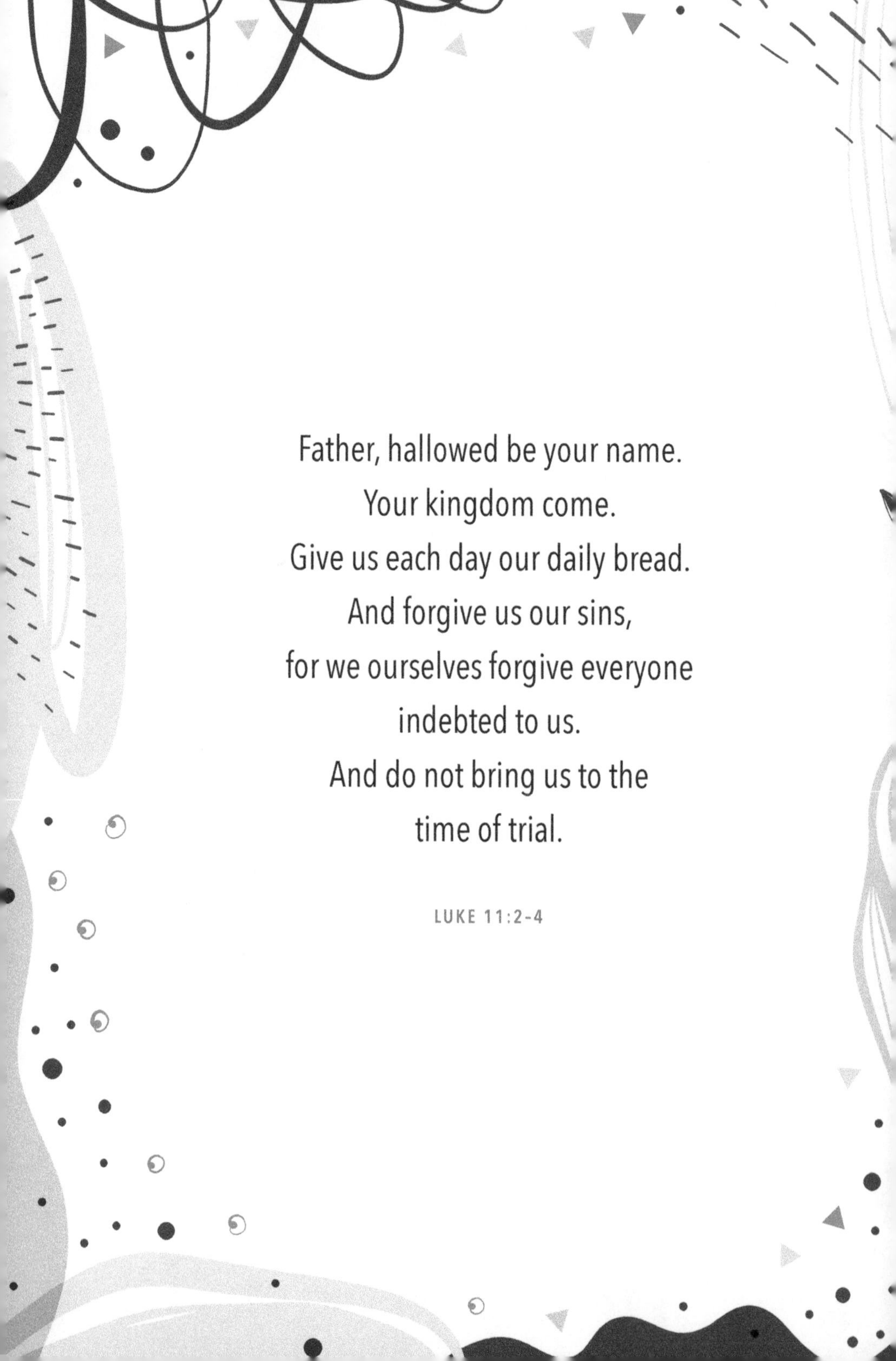

Father, hallowed be your name.
Your kingdom come.
Give us each day our daily bread.
And forgive us our sins,
for we ourselves forgive everyone
indebted to us.
And do not bring us to the
time of trial.

LUKE 11:2-4

WHAT IS PRAYER?

One of the great mysteries of 2014 was the disappearance of Malaysia Airlines Flight 370 with 239 people on board. Many days into the search, an Australian military officer got on television to outline the next steps. He basically asked us all to pray. He asked us to pray that God would lead them to the plane.

When the interview ended, the newscasters seemed slightly dumbfounded. Finally one of them said, “We have moved to a new phase where clearly we have very few options left if the military officers are asking us to pray.” I understood what he was saying. When the people we count on for action and results are telling us the best option at this point is prayer, it does feel like we are running out of options.

I have always believed that prayer is a practice that we need more than a practice that God requires. I have never been able to believe that God refuses to intervene in life because you or I have not said a prayer. Instead, I’ve come to understand the power of prayer as a practice that helps us reconnect with the sacred centeredness in us, the quiet place where God can speak and we can hear. Connecting to that sacred space day after day over the span of a lifetime changes the way we live and move and have our being in the world. Prayer changes us; it doesn’t change God.

But I also believe that we have the capacity, through prayer, to tap into a larger energy source (I call that God) where we can collectively channel love so powerfully that it can change the world precisely because it changes the way we live. I believe we can literally create heaven on earth just as dependably as we have created hell on earth.

Does this sound crazy? As I reread this, I think perhaps it does. Yet my life speaks to its truth. Prayer has changed the way I live and imagine possibilities for our shared life together. But something more powerful happens for me when I am living prayerfully—much like awakening to a sixth sense. You can sense a nonjudgmental energy guiding you, urging you on, coaxing you into working toward all of creation’s wholeness.

I'm still not sure what finally I believe about prayer. I don't know that praying will help us find a plane in a vast ocean. But I do know that the more I ground myself in this beautiful practice, the more comfortable I become in my own skin and the more assured I am that we have capacities for goodness far beyond what we know.

Give it a try today. Try again tomorrow. Maybe even try it the next day. As the Australian military officer reminds us, if you have tried everything else in your search, maybe it's time for a new phase. Let's pray.

REFLECT

What do you believe about prayer? What do you think it does for you and in the world?

Write a prayer that you feel in your bones, one that comes from your heart. Let's see what changes for you.

Who teaches us more than
the animals of the earth,
and makes us wiser than
the birds of the air?

JOB 35:11

WHAT STORIES ARE YOU TELLING?

A friend recently told me a story about her grandmother, Bobba, who spent time with her as a little girl. They would often go out in the mornings to feed the birds together. Looking back now, she sees that these moments, more than many others in her life, shaped her.

She said, "We didn't just throw food out and go on with our day. Bobba taught me to pause and really see the birds. I learned their distinct calls. I knew their breeds. And then often Bobba would tell me something about myself through stories about the birds. She told me that I could fly like them, creating an adventurous life for myself. She taught me about fear, creativity, bravery, love, and compassion through these small life lessons. I am who I am today because of Bobba and her stories."

My friend is now "Bobba" for her own grandchildren, and the beautiful stories continue.

As Jesus walked the countryside with his followers, I imagine it was a lot like my friend learning to feed the birds. They walked and talked and, in the process, became more beautifully whole and fully human.

We need more "Bobbas" in the world. Maybe that is you. We need people who know how to see what matters and take the time to show the rest of us. For the rest of us, we must slow down enough to listen closely. Stories take time to incubate within us and ultimately to transform us into something new.

REFLECT

What stories have shaped who you have become as a woman?

What stories would you tell younger women about the journey of growing wise as a woman?

CLOSING PRAYER

Lord God,
Grant me the wisdom to know the
story to which you have called me
and the courage to live it as my own.
Grant me also the willingness to
share what I learn with others, that
they may learn more of you by
my walking in your ways.
Amen.

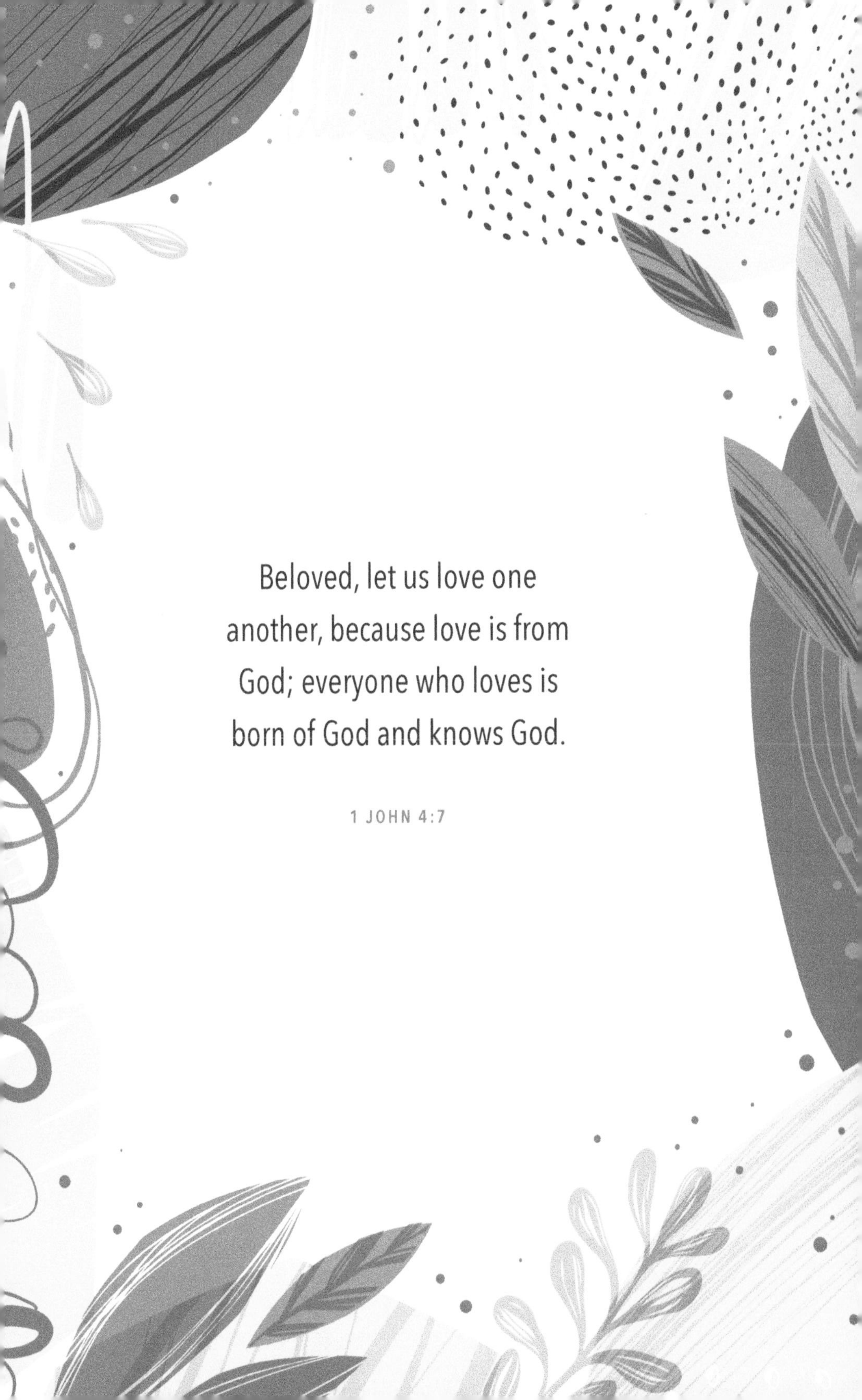

Beloved, let us love one another, because love is from God; everyone who loves is born of God and knows God.

1 JOHN 4:7

ON LOVING ONE ANOTHER

Several years ago I saw the movie *Wit*, a Mike Nichols film starring Emma Thompson. The movie is about Dr. Vivian Bearing, a first-rate scholar specializing in 17th-century English literature, especially the poetry of John Donne. Vivian had a biting wit, which educated but also alienated her students. She had poured her life into becoming a scholar without peer. Her life was in control, and she needed nothing, she thought, other than her scholarship and her career.

Then Vivian was diagnosed with a rare form of ovarian cancer. She was confronted with a life situation for which all her scholarship had not prepared her. She no longer had all the answers—and she was no longer in control.

The usual treatments would not work, so she entered a teaching and research hospital and agreed to experimental treatments. For eight months, she underwent treatments that were painful and humiliating and the outcomes of which were uncertain. She was no longer a teacher but a *subject* for others to study. Her doctors gave her the best medical treatment but no human warmth. In a moment of despair, Vivian reflected that she thought being smart would be enough. But then it became clear: Basic human kindness was all that mattered in the end.

One day, toward the end of the movie, Vivian's teacher, the one under whom she had done her doctoral work, came to see her. The elderly scholar tried to comfort her but clearly was unsure of what to do. "I'll recite something by Donne," she said, but Vivian vehemently said no. Looking around as if lost, the professor saw the bag of books she had bought for her grandchild's birthday. She took a child's book from the bag, got up on the bed with Vivian, and held her in her arms while she read *The Runaway Bunny*. These two eminent scholars were comforted by a child's book about a mother bunny who assures her child that she will pursue him wherever he goes because he is her little bunny.

Of course, when you hear it with the ears of faith, you know the book is really about a God whose love will never let us go, wherever we are and whatever we are going through. By holding her tenderly and reading the simple story of unfailing love, the professor helps Vivian drift into a peaceful sleep. What amazing love.

Is that what it's about? At the end of the day, it is about love: first God's and then ours.

REFLECT

What memories from your own life did this story bring up for you?

"Come to me, all you
that are weary and are
carrying heavy burdens,
and I will give you rest."

MATTHEW 11:28

A BUSY LIFE

Women are pros at the "busy" game. We generally have a hard time saying no. We want to be a great boss, parent, employee, spouse, friend, daughter, socialite, entrepreneur, fitness fanatic, and so on. Even crazier, we do all these things because we are chasing some illusive sense of balance. The crisis this creates for us is absolute exhaustion. When we hear Jesus say the phrase in the Gospel of Matthew, most of us actually cry with relief. We are desperate for rest.

Businesswoman Randi Zuckerberg was being interviewed on a panel when the moderator asked the infamous "work/life balance" question. "Randi," he began, "you are a mom, *and* you have a career. How do you balance it all?"

She had answered it 100 times before with platitudes about how much help she had and how hard she worked. But this time, frustrated to answer this question one more time, she finally told her truth. "I don't," she said. "In order to set myself up for success, I know I can only realistically do *three* things well every day. So, every day when I wake up, I think to myself: Work. Sleep. Family. Friends. Fitness. Pick three." It's good advice.

Over the past year, I have stopped glorifying busyness. I have rejected the frantic anxiety it produces, the excuses I started to make for my missteps because I was moving too fast and doing too much. In that process, I made an important discovery: I was hiding behind my busyness so that I didn't have to take responsibility for bringing my best work into the world. I was just too busy, I told myself, to do the deep work, the scary work, the meaning-making work of owning my contribution to our world.

If you are really busy, heading into each weekend ready to collapse, ask yourself if you might be hiding from your own potential. It happens to the best of us.

REFLECT

Do you believe work/life balance is essential for a happy life?

How do you know when you are burning out?

CLOSING PRAYER

Lord God,
Remind me that I am enough
without having to be all things
to all people. I deserve to be
healthy, to have time to myself,
and to rest when I need it. Help
me remember that I am not failing
when I decide to slow down. In fact,
I might actually be living in closer
communion with you.
Amen.

For all of us make many mistakes. Anyone who makes no mistakes in speaking is perfect, able to keep the whole body in check with a bridle.

JAMES 3:2

WE ALL MAKE MISTAKES

I live in fear of making mistakes. Sometimes I say things I don't mean to say, or I don't say things that should be said. Sometimes I fail to do things I said that I would. Sometimes I do things I shouldn't do. It's often hard for me to forgive myself when I fail.

We all make mistakes in our words and actions. None of us is perfect. In this passage, James invites us to consider that we have enormous power, and therefore responsibility, to speak and act with kindness and honesty. We can change someone's life with a kind word, and we can break their heart with hateful words.

Think about the kindest words that anyone has ever spoken to you. What difference did they make for you? Now consider the most painful words someone has said to you. What impact did they have?

Our words have such power because they shape our reality. When we are young, our parents and siblings might speak about us without much intention. We often believe what they say and live out their opinions of us. If someone tells you as a little girl that you are smart, you may make better grades and embrace more ambitious goals in your life. But if someone tells you that you aren't very smart and you believe them, you may struggle to overcome that belief for much of your life.

The same holds true for how you speak and act as an adult. You have enormous power to encourage people in your life. You can speak words of hope and healing into them. You can inspire them to dream bigger dreams for themselves than they dared to dream on their own. Or you can speak words that hold them back.

None of us is perfect with our words all the time. We will make mistakes, and we all pay the same price. James goes on in this passage to say that you can't say false things about people and praise God with the same tongue. In other words, we can't live with integrity if we aren't mindful of our words and actions. Today, pay attention to how you speak and act as expressions of God's love moving through you. It might change someone's life. It is guaranteed to change yours.

REFLECT

When has someone said something kind or powerful to you and it changed the course of your life?

Who could you offer support to in your network that might need encouragement to keep trying?

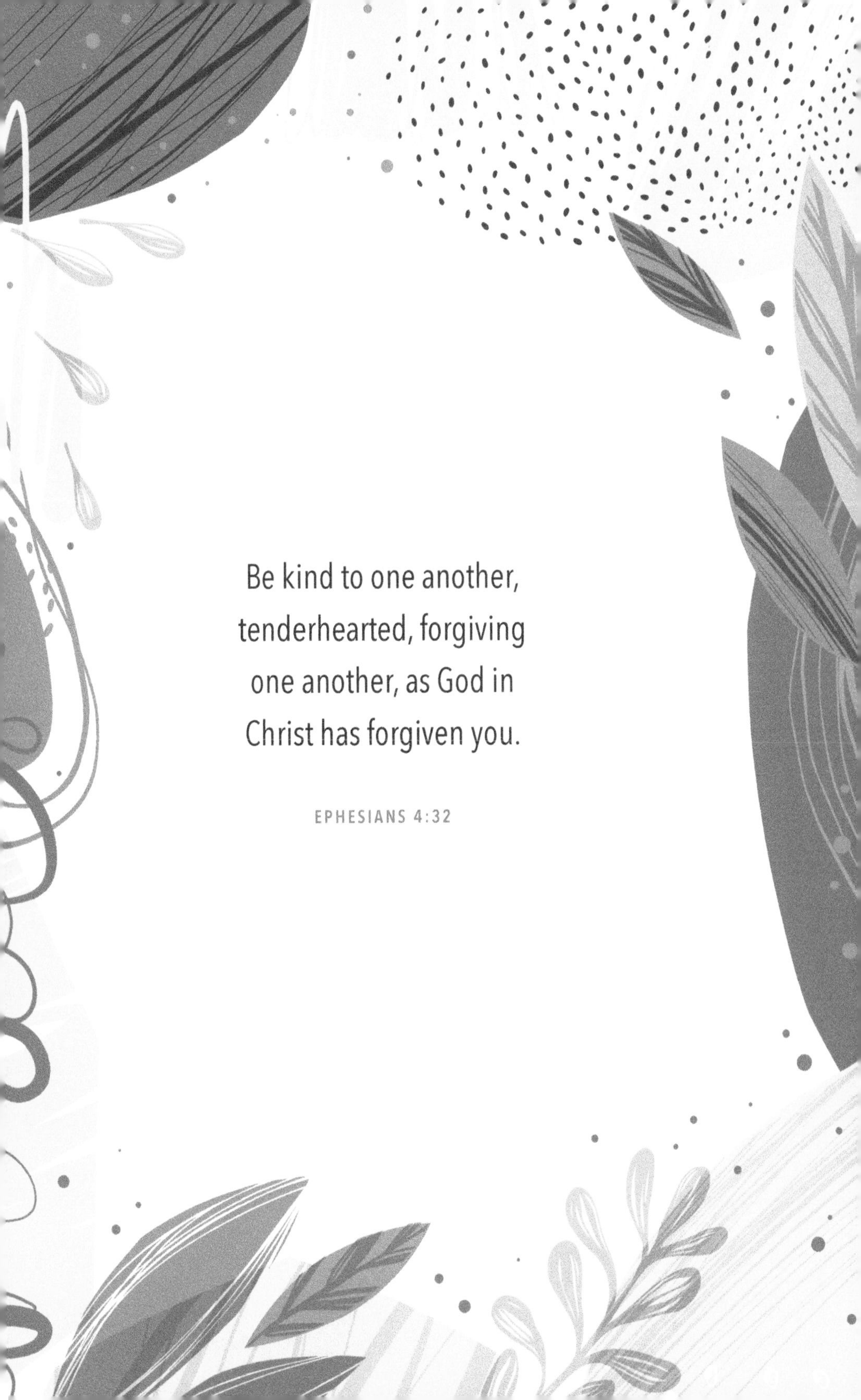

Be kind to one another,
tenderhearted, forgiving
one another, as God in
Christ has forgiven you.

EPHESIANS 4:32

BE KIND TO YOURSELF

I have a hard time forgiving myself. I can easily forgive you if you make a mistake. If you say something harsh or fail to deliver on a promise, I can get over that. But if I make a mistake or fail to do something that I promised to do, I will beat myself up for days. Most of us are not good with our own failures.

Fear of failing is one of the greatest barriers to our chancing success. It also feeds our anxiety, stress, and depression when we allow it to claim our mental and emotional energy. I can remember long nights early in my career when I would wake up in a panic, afraid that I had forgotten a meeting or that we would run out of money and not be able to pay our staff. I remember fearing what others would think of me. I worried that I wasn't smart enough or strong enough or kind enough.

Here are 20 ways that we imagine failure:

- Humiliated
- Embarrassed
- Expelled
- Defunded
- Typos found
- Defeated
- Fired
- Called out
- Unappreciated
- Late
- Found out
- Mocked
- Outclassed
- Criticized
- Out of cash
- In debt
- Underdressed
- Out of tune
- Out of your league
- Unprepared

I look back on my early years struggling with my fear of failing, and I smile. No one could have changed those experiences—they are part of growing up for most of us—but now I think, "What a waste of time." I know that we all fear failure. But that doesn't mean we get to quit. It just means we get to be generous with each other—because we are all vulnerable and courageous, usually at the same time. If you fall short of your goals, forgive yourself just as you forgive others. It's the only way to stay in the creative game and the only way to make a real difference.

REFLECT

What gifts has failure brought you?

What mistakes have you made in your words or actions with others that you still need to forgive yourself for?

CLOSING PRAYER

Forgive yourself for not knowing
better at the time.
Forgive yourself for giving
away your power.
Forgive yourself for past behaviors.
Forgive yourself for the survival
patterns and traits you picked up
while enduring trauma.
Forgive yourself for being who
you needed to be.
—Audrey Kitching

And the one who was seated on the throne said, "See, I am making all things new." Also he said, "Write this, for these words are trustworthy and true."

REVELATION 21:5

A SEVENTH STORY

My friend and colleague Brian McLaren has cowritten an important book called *Cory and the Seventh Story*. It's a children's book that adults need to read. Most of us know that the stories we tell ourselves shape our understanding of the world. As Brian and his coauthor, Gareth Higgins, point out, we have told ourselves six stories as a nation all grounded in a myth of redemptive violence.

- The first story is the *domination* story where "we" rule over "them."
- The second story is the *revolution* story where we take revenge over them.
- The third story is the *purification* story where we, the majority, blame them, the minority, for our struggles and exclude or exterminate them.
- The fourth story is the *victimization* story that justifies our actions through the scale of our pain.
- The fifth story is the *isolation* story where we withdraw from society, believing in our own righteousness, and look for a promised land.
- The sixth story is the *accumulation* story, which pretends that happiness comes from having stuff and making sure no one can steal our stuff.

The trouble with these stories is that they depend on violence to stay in existence. We continue to believe and act as if the world was designed to bring order from chaos *out of force*. It is "us" versus "them."

I don't believe this message has ever made sense to women. We know somewhere deep within us that it doesn't work. Violence doesn't create peace. Killing does not redeem or cleanse. Hoarding does not guarantee happiness.

There is a better way. A way of Love. It a story of reconciliation and liberation.

I won't give away the ending, the seventh story. All I ask for today is that you pay attention to the stories that are influencing your life. Becoming aware is the first step to becoming free.

REFLECT

Think about the movies you watch and the television shows you invest in. What stories are they telling you about the world?

Can you imagine a story of the world where people live at peace? How would you tell it?

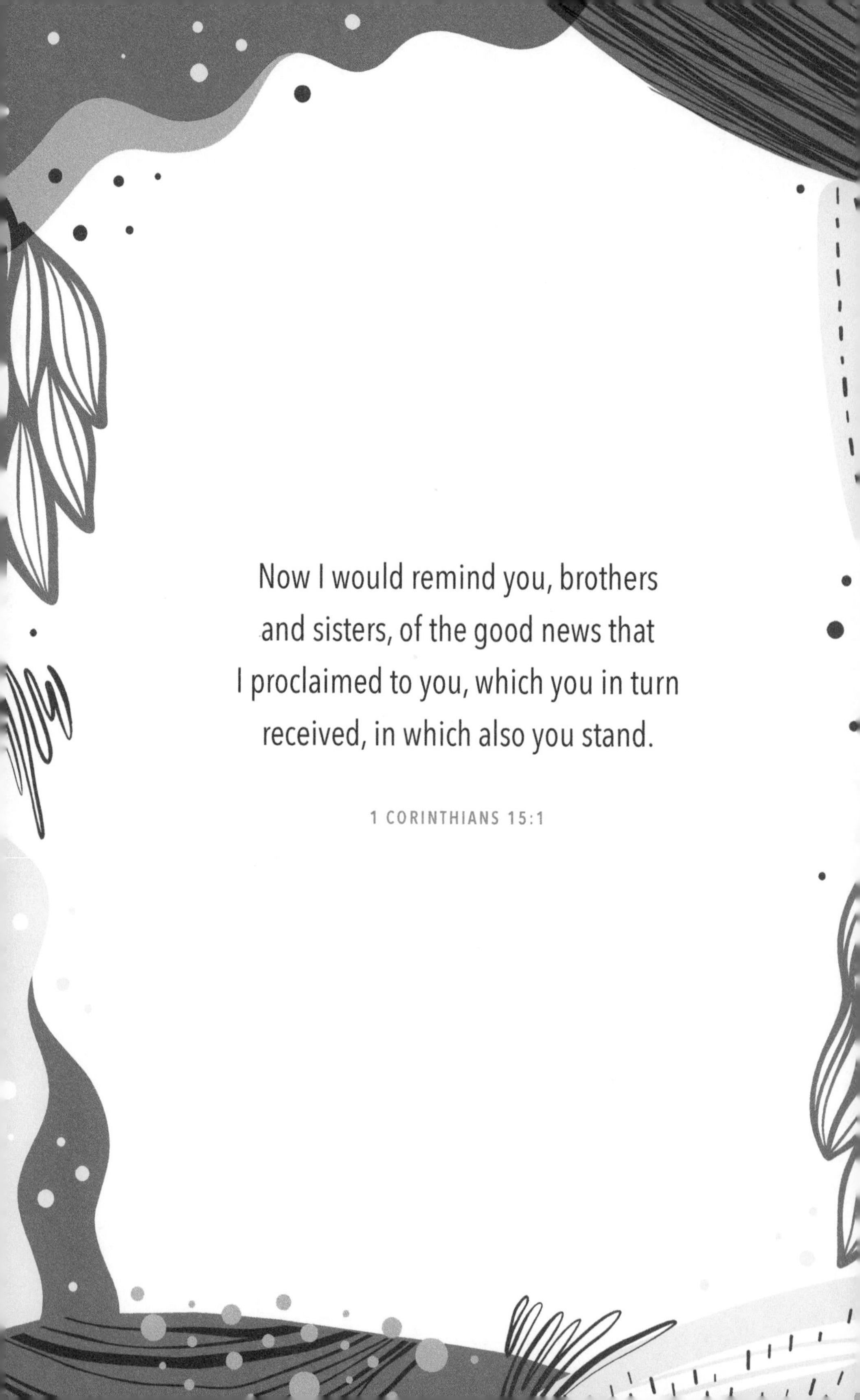

Now I would remind you, brothers
and sisters, of the good news that
I proclaimed to you, which you in turn
received, in which also you stand.

1 CORINTHIANS 15:1

PROVING OUR WORTH

In this passage from 1 Corinthians, Paul is reminding the people of Corinth that by being followers of God, they stand in a new identity. They don't need to prove that identity to anyone else. It is simply gifted by the fact that they know and accept themselves as children of God.

Identity is a complicated concept these days. When I walk through the TSA security line in the airport, I have to prove my identity by showing my photo ID or passport. When I purchase something on credit, I have to prove that my credit history makes me worthy of a loan. When I apply for a job, I have to prove my credentials. That is true for all of us. Our identities are our modern currency telling the rest of the world who we are, what jobs we are credentialed to do, where we can live, what resources we can access, what software we can use, and where we can travel.

Our identities can also be questioned. As a woman, when I stand on a stage, I feel like I have to prove that I deserve to be there. When I offer my son's coach a suggestion about strategy, I feel like I have to prove I know what I am talking about. When I sit in the captain seat of an airplane, I feel the pressure of proving that I am in command of the flight.

Women must prove a lot to have influence in the world. Our identities as women are tested as we move through the world with more confidence and assertiveness. Often, the same is true about our identities as Christians. But our worthiness as women and as children of God is not for anyone to determine but ourselves. You don't owe anyone proof of your inherent worth.

REFLECT

From where do you gain a sense of worth? From other people? From yourself? From God?

CLOSING PRAYER

May your sense of being be
rooted in who you are,
not as much by what you do.
May you stand in the knowledge
that you are God's daughter,
And you are enough.
Amen.

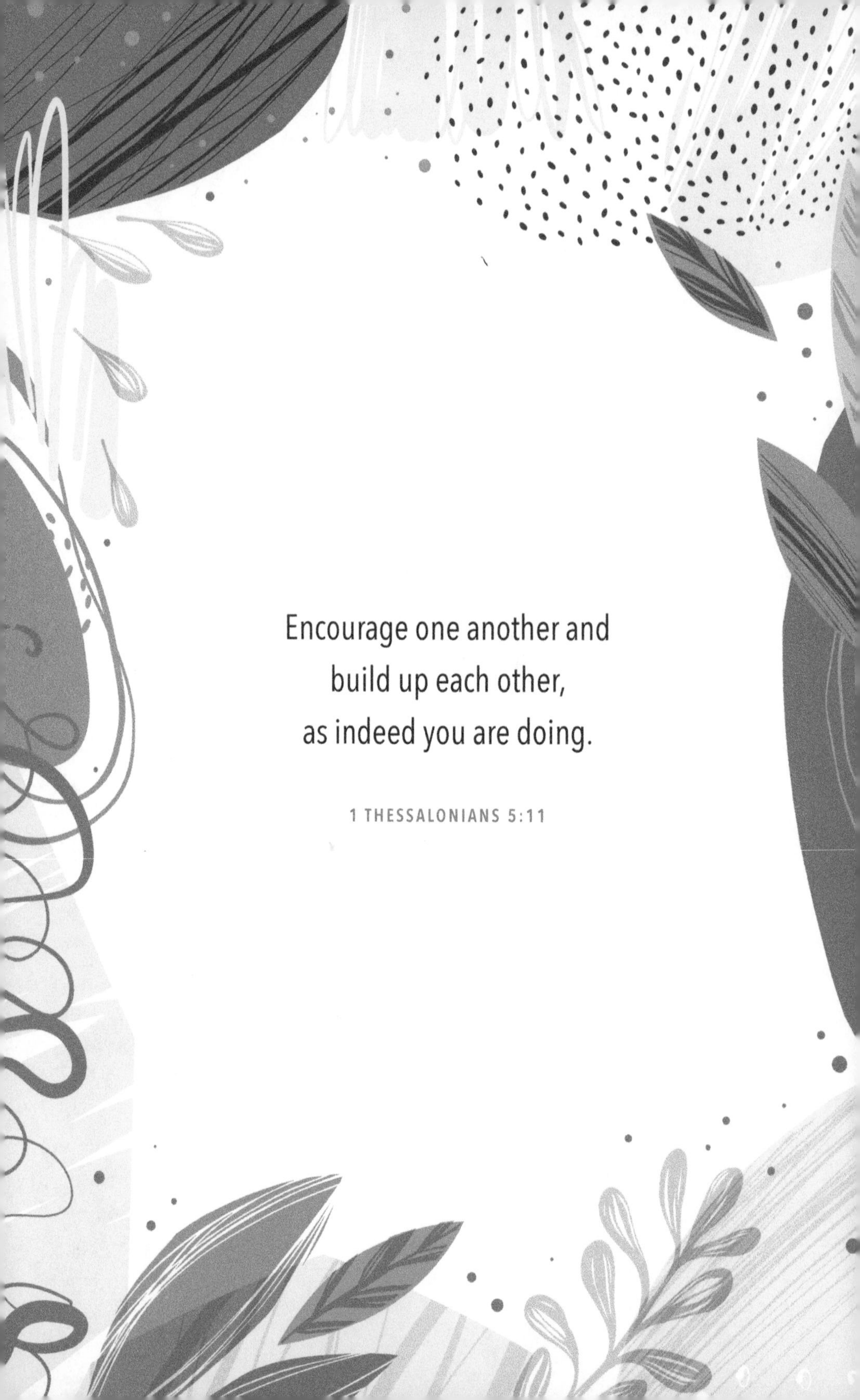

Encourage one another and
build up each other,
as indeed you are doing.

1 THESSALONIANS 5:11

YOU DON'T HAVE TO DO IT ALONE

During the early years of Christianity, people who were new to the faith faced a number of challenges. They would often become discouraged and confused. Much of the New Testament is letters written by the Apostle Paul offering encouragement to these communities. In 1 Thessalonians, he expresses this hope that they support one another most clearly. Life is difficult; we need each other to help us thrive.

I recently read a book that I loved called *Maybe You Should Talk to Someone* by Lori Gottlieb. She is a psychotherapist who tells stories of her conversations with her own therapists and then with some of her patients. She is hilarious. If you have ever been in a therapy session, you will completely relate.

What I love about this book is that it is normalizing mental health support. She offers wonderful advice for all of us, like "There's no hierarchy of pain. Suffering shouldn't be ranked, because pain is not a contest." My personal favorite is when she observes that when the present falls apart, so does the future we had associated with it. Having the future taken away is the mother of all plot twists.

For the people of Thessalonica, just like us today, their present changed when they learned about Jesus and the God he talked about. They had to reorient their entire understanding of what mattered in life. It created disruptions and confusion because they were having to let go of one way of living and embrace a new vision of the future. It was a much better vision for their future. But it was different, and change is hard. They needed to encourage one another because that kind of "futuring" is hard work to do.

All of us are doing that work all the time. Our present is changing all the time, and we are having to simultaneously let go of the future connected to it and reimagine a new one. It can be stressful, and talking to others helps. You don't have to be on the edge of a complete breakdown to benefit from talking to someone. Just like going to the gym makes our bodies stronger, talking to a psychotherapist makes our minds and souls stronger. I am a big fan.

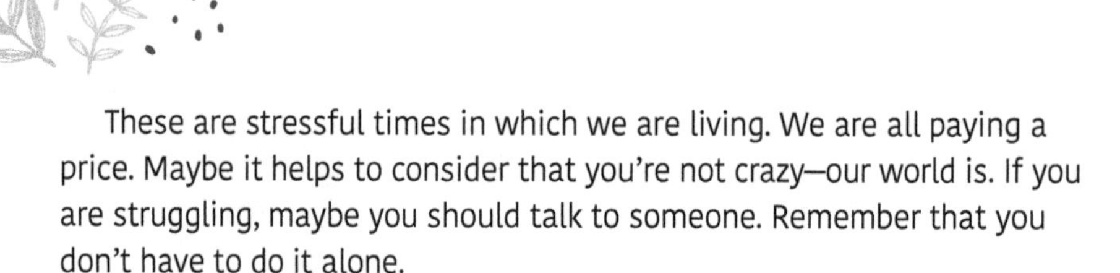

These are stressful times in which we are living. We are all paying a price. Maybe it helps to consider that you're not crazy—our world is. If you are struggling, maybe you should talk to someone. Remember that you don't have to do it alone.

REFLECT

Have you ever worked with a therapist? What was that experience like for you?

When you feel stressed or anxious, do you feel like you have the support you need to get through it?

People were bringing little children to him in order that he might touch them; and the disciples spoke sternly to them. But when Jesus saw this, he was indignant and said to them, "Let the little children come to me; do not stop them; for it is to such as these that the kingdom of God belongs. Truly I tell you, whoever does not receive the kingdom of God as a little child will never enter it." And he took them up in his arms, laid his hands on them, and blessed them.

MARK 10:13-16

LET THE CHILDREN COME

Caring for the young ones in our community is a sacred calling for all of us, including those of us who have not birthed our own. When Jesus saw children, he welcomed them to him without hesitation because he knew that their innocence and tenderness are the closest experience we may ever have of heaven. Children are precious gifts. We are all responsible for caring for, tending, loving, and shaping the young.

Children help remind us that:

- Our capacity to love is breathtaking and endless.
- A single smile can change everything wrong in our day.
- We think we are in control, but we are not.
- We were never meant to parent alone; we need a tribe to raise a child.

A friend of mine recently had a baby, a beautiful little girl whose presence in this world brings me joy. I feel a bit better about our world just because she is now in it. Actually, I feel that way about all of our children. They are our greatest teachers.

Jesus said that whoever does not receive the kingdom of God with the spirit of a little child will never enter it. Children are open, nonjudgmental, and curious. They don't need to critique what is offered to them by the rest of us. They simply trust that we are there for their goodness, and they welcome us with open arms.

Jesus wants us to approach our relationship to God with the same open spirit. When we do, we will feel the embrace of God's unconditional love, not because it wasn't there before but because we are finally open to receiving it.

REFLECT

Beyond your immediate family, who cared for you growing up?

Who do you "mother" today? What is precious about that experience for you?

CLOSING PRAYER

May you be open to the wisdom
and love offered by all ages but
especially attentive to the children.
Learn to see the world through the
innocence of their eyes and celebrate
the hope you find in them.
Amen.

I am about to do a new thing;
now it springs forth, do you
not perceive it?
I will make a way in
the wilderness and
rivers in the desert.

ISAIAH 43:19

A CREATIVE LIFE

I'm convinced that we are living in the midst of an awakening of our wild souls. Some of us, whom I've come to call Wisdom Warriors, sense a new level of creativity emerging in ourselves—one that leads us on the healing path to a deeper awareness of the creative force that is within.

Every woman has a source of wild creativity in her. We are built to give birth, to bring things, ideas, and people to life. At our deepest core, we are created to write, sing, dance, and love new life into being. We are born wild, in tune with our intuitions of how to make a more beautiful world.

All too early in life, our domesticated elders tell us to tame this wild creativity. We might become too creative, too generative, too free. We might test social boundaries or question authority. We might get arrogant or too sure of ourselves or discover we're more powerful than even we knew. We are told from a young age to hold back, to moderate, to question our ability to contribute from our wild and wise ways. If you follow this advice, it kills your soul.

I love this passage from Isaiah for this reason. As the story goes, he received a revelation from God and, following God's instructions, walked around naked for three years declaring the coming of the Lord. He didn't care what people thought. He had a message to deliver and strong enough sense of himself to deliver it with a flash (pun intended). I'm not advocating that any of us walk around naked in public, but I am suggesting that it takes a certain internal freedom to have the courage to even imagine it.

If you are a Wisdom Warrior, take solace in knowing you aren't "crazy"—the world is. Keep making your way in the wilderness, moving forward with the truth you know in the deepest parts of your soul. It's your authentic wildness, not your conformity, that the world really needs.

REFLECT

How do you see yourself differently if you think of yourself as a Wisdom Warrior?

What holds you back from living in that "wild and free" space within yourself more?

For all must carry
their own loads.

GALATIANS 6:5

BOUNDARIES

In the early church, people were trying to figure out how to live in community together. Based on what they had learned from their time with Jesus, they built a community where everything was shared in common. Families sold their properties and gave the proceeds to the community. In turn, they and their families were cared for. But building community this way meant people had a vested interest in everything being fair. Sometimes arguments would break out about who was doing too little to help the others.

Paul, the writer of Galatians, sensed that they needed a clearer sense of boundaries, so he wrote them a letter in which he told them to bear one another's burdens and "carry their own loads." What he was trying to say is that families work best when everyone carries responsibilities in equal measure, preventing any one person from being hurt by doing too much or too little.

I am still learning about these things called "boundaries." People have mentioned them to me over the years, and I thought they were in place to keep us from doing illegal or unethical things. Now I realize they can also keep us from doing soul-killing, life-taking things. They also help us live in healthy relationship with one another.

Prentis Hemphill said, "Boundaries are the distance at which I can love you and me simultaneously." YES!

Many women struggle with establishing boundaries. We want to serve everyone and everything—our families, our colleagues, our church, our community, our friends, the friends of our friends, the strangers we meet on the street, the stray dog who shows up at our door. We often give until we have little left, and we burn out. But that isn't ever what God asks of us. If we want to be healthy, we have to carry our own load and no one else's.

Given the pressure and stress in most of our lives, knowing our boundaries seems essential to knowing ourselves. We can't possibly do soul-level work if we are sacrificing our sanity in the process.

REFLECT

What boundaries have you set in your life that make the most difference?

How do you know when your boundaries, the rules you have in place to protect yourself and others, are being tested or compromised?

CLOSING PRAYER

May you have the sense
within yourself
to know your genuine “yes”
and your honest “no.”
May you hold fast to your
deepest sense of YOU
so that the rest of us
might respect who you truly are.
Amen.

Now his elder son was in the field; and when he came and approached the house, he heard music and dancing. He called one of the [servants] and asked what was going on. He replied, "Your brother has come, and your father has killed the fatted calf, because he has got him back safe and sound." Then he became angry and refused to go in. . . . Then the father said to him, "Son, you are always with me, and all that is mine is yours. But we had to celebrate and rejoice, because this brother of yours was dead and has come to life; he was lost and has been found."

LUKE 15:25–28, 31–32

THE DRAMA TRIANGLE

Recently I was working with an organization where I interviewed key leaders about their roles. I soon noticed a common theme that went something like this:

1. This person/decision/experience hurt me.
2. This person/decision/experience rescued me.
3. I am here only until I am hurt again—then I am gone.

These people were reflecting real pain, but their pain became predictable because they were the victims of persecutors. They waited to be rescued, until someone or something came along and made them feel better. But they were waiting for an injury to happen again.

It's the "drama triangle." If you want to play the role of the victim, you have to have a persecutor and a rescuer. Otherwise, it doesn't work.

So many of us live in this space of feeling victimized by people or events in our lives. We give up our power, waiting to be rescued, while we sit in our pain.

The story of the prodigal son is a well-known story about a son who wastes his inheritance from his father on partying and foolish living and then comes home after many years to ask for forgiveness and return to his family. What we don't focus on so much is the experience of the older brother who stayed and worked to support his parents. When he hears that the younger brother has returned, and the father is throwing a huge party, the older son is angry. His argument goes like this:

1. I've been the good son. I sacrificed when my brother left. (He hurt me.)
2. You should not throw him a party! You should see my sacrifice and honor me instead. (Fix this situation for me.)
3. I can't believe this. Why should I keep working this hard if this is what my brother gets? (I'm out of here.)

Maybe you've lived this pattern in your life—I certainly have in mine. What shall we do?

The most resilient people I know experience pain, too. But then they do something unusual: They turn it into something creative. Prosecutors become challengers. Rescuers become coaches. In this way, you hold your power. You grow instead of shrink. You move forward instead of getting stuck in the past. You focus on outcomes instead of problems. You live in peace instead of strife.

REFLECT

Everyone gets caught in drama triangles from time to time. Think about a time in your life when you were clearly playing the role of the victim. How did that serve you?

What would you do differently in that situation today?

The word that came to Jeremiah from the Lord:
"Come, go down to the potter's house,
and there I will let you hear my words."
So I went down to the potter's house,
and there he was working at his wheel.
The vessel he was making of clay was
spoiled in the potter's hand, and he reworked
it into another vessel, as seemed
good to him.

JEREMIAH 18:1-4

AN UNLIVED LIFE

Living a creative life takes enormous courage. While we all need creative expression, women often use art to connect to the deeper parts of ourselves. We connect to our vulnerability and our beauty. It takes guts to go there for most of us. Especially because when we are creative and then have the courage to show our creations to others, we open ourselves to their critique. They may love what we offer into the world; they may hate it. We have to be prepared for either reaction, though I will encourage you to consider that neither actually matters in the end.

Women who are deeply creative can also fall into the trap of hiding their true gifts. It is tempting for any of us to hide, to never show others what we are capable of contributing. In this way, we save ourselves from possible embarrassment and heartbreak.

The price we pay is an unactualized life. Our epitaph might read, "We sensed she came into this world with unique gifts, but she took her best work with her."

We are lucky to have this passage from Jeremiah to remind us that, as the artists we all are, we are not called to perfection. We don't have to create anything in the world that everyone loves. In fact, we can't. But we do have to show up in our own "potter's house" and try our best to create works that are unique to us and might inspire others. It might be literal art, or it might be strong relationships, a healthy family, a growing company, a winning soccer team, a popular blog, a store on Etsy, a knitted sweater, a new degree, a computer program, or a community play.

You have a contribution to make to the world that only *you* can make. The rest of us are waiting, with hope, to see what that will be.

REFLECT

Imagine that you are going to your own "potter's house." What is the first thing you want to create when you get there?

What would you create if you knew it didn't have to be perfect?

CLOSING PRAYER

Lord God,
I sense that I have creativity ready to burst forth from me. I am often scared to honor that. I worry about what my friends and family might think. Give me courage this day to make the time. Give me tenacity to engage my creativity. Give me hope to know that you have been here too, shaping and molding me, so you can show me the way.
Amen.

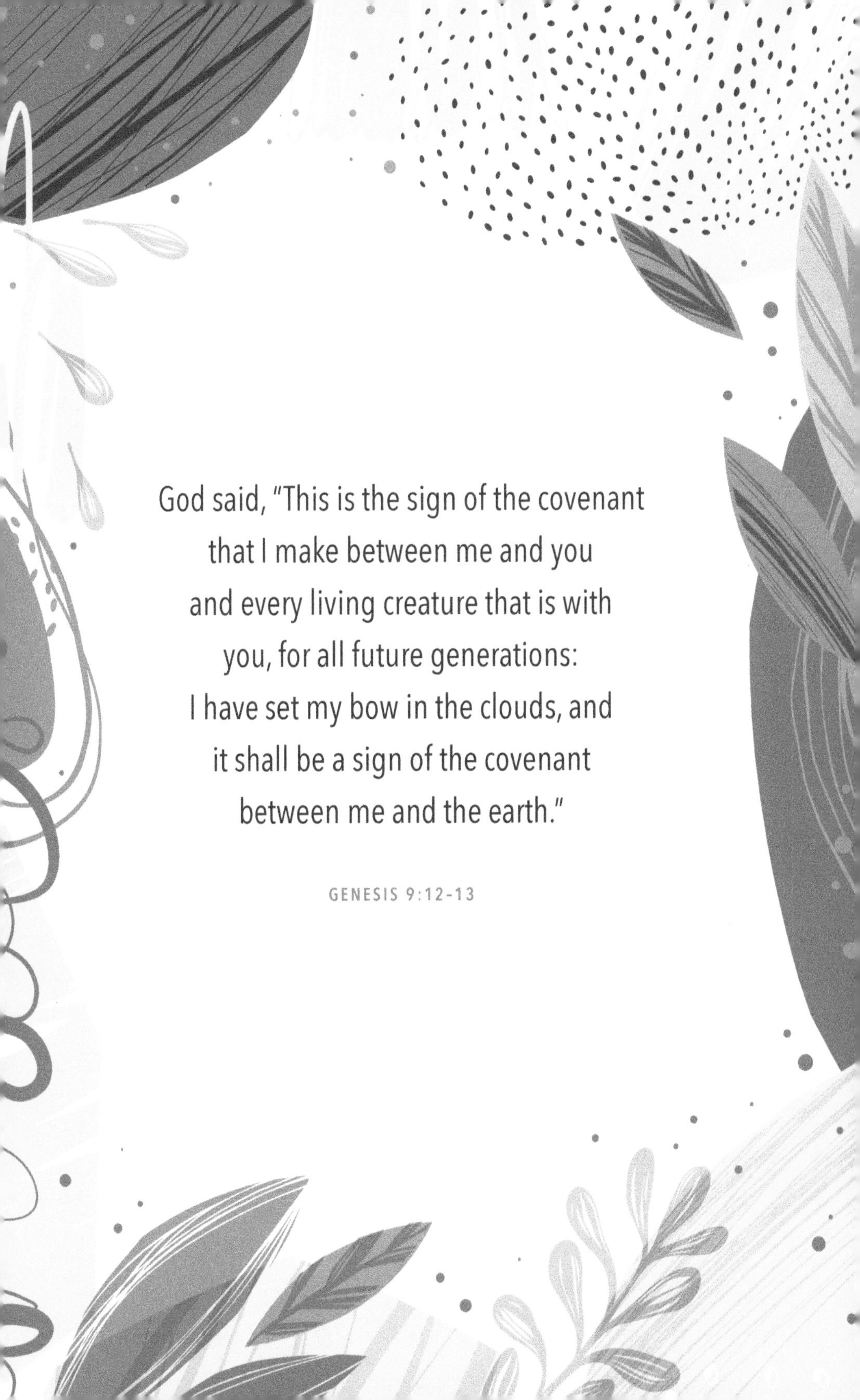

God said, "This is the sign of the covenant
that I make between me and you
and every living creature that is with
you, for all future generations:
I have set my bow in the clouds, and
it shall be a sign of the covenant
between me and the earth."

GENESIS 9:12-13

OVER THE RAINBOW

As I descended into Atlanta's Hartsfield-Jackson International Airport, I looked out the window to see a stunning rainbow arching across the sky. You could clearly see all of the colors blending together harmoniously. It was glorious!

Rainbows always give me hope. In the Old Testament, when Noah saw the rainbow in the sky after the Great Flood, it was the sign that it was safe to emerge from the ark. But it was also a sign that the only world he had ever known had been washed away. He would be walking out into a brand-new world. In this way, the rainbow is a transition point, a doorway to new possibilities.

So many of us are hurting right now. So many of us are struggling with addictions and anxiety and stress and emotional exhaustion and traumas. It becomes easy to lose hope. It becomes easy to think we are going to be endlessly stuck in the Great Flood of pain that we are tempted to give up and succumb. I understand that.

But then a rainbow appears. A doorway of hope opens. A friend shows up. A job comes through. An intervention happens. A person offers forgiveness. A treatment works. An unexpected check comes in the mail. A donation is made. Hope becomes REAL.

You have to be prepared to embrace the new world and new possibilities in order to emerge from the ark of pain and loss, grief, and unknowing. No one can take that step for you. It's yours to claim for yourself. It may be the hardest and bravest thing you have ever done in your life.

Here is what I do know: a wonderful world awaits us on the other side of pain. God's promise to us was never that we would live lives free of pain. We are free beings and as such are capable of creating great pain for ourselves and others. God values our freedom enough to tolerate our suffering. But God's promise was that we would never be alone. God is always there, hoping for our healing and our wholeness.

If you are feeling devastated by the mess of the world or the mess of your life, I hope you will keep your eyes aimed toward the sky. The rainbows are there. The new world awaits. You have every reason to hope, if you have the courage to say “yes.”

REFLECT

In what ways do you feel hopeless and powerless in your life?

What do you need to say “yes” to in order to claim the possibility of a new life?

When the sabbath was over, Mary Magdalene, and Mary the mother of James, and Salome bought spices, so that they might go and anoint him. . . . As they entered the tomb, they saw a young man, dressed in a white robe, sitting on the right side; and they were alarmed. But he said to them, "Do not be alarmed; you are looking for Jesus of Nazareth, who was crucified. He has been raised; he is not here. . . ." So they went out and fled from the tomb, for terror and amazement had seized them; and they said nothing to anyone, for they were afraid.

MARK 16:1, 5-6, 8

DANCING WITH HEARTBREAK AND HOPE

It's interesting that all four Gospel accounts of the resurrection are different. They are all talking about the same experience, but each writer has a very different take on what happened. For Mark, the resurrection was the end of the story. He ends with, *"So they went out and fled from the tomb, for terror and amazement had seized them; and they said nothing to anyone, for they were afraid."* Later, people thought that was too abrupt an ending, so someone added a few verses on at the end to say something along the lines of "But then they did talk, and word spread, and Jesus reappeared, and then he ascended into heaven, and we should keep up the good work."

The other Gospels all have their own takes on what happened. It would have been easy to harmonize the stories, especially since they were written so many years after the resurrection experience. But they are so different—I suppose that is to be expected when you experience a major event in life. We may all have a shared experience, but we would tell the story differently.

I love that because it means we can tell the story of resurrection in our lives in ways that feel most authentic to us. We all know about resurrection—the time you lost your job and then got an even better one. Or the heartbreak of going through a divorce only to discover a strength in yourself that you didn't know you had. Or those years when you are trying to survive your teenage children and then they grow up to be decent human beings who can pay their own bills. We know about resurrection because we also know about crucifixion. They go together.

As you consider what death and resurrection mean to you, play with telling the stories of both through the lessons from your own life, when you were dancing with both heartbreak and hope. It's in the telling of our own stories that we find new life.

REFLECT

Life is based on a sacred cycle: life, death, life again. How has that been true in your life?

CLOSING PRAYER

Lord God,
In every place we encounter
persecution and death,
may we remember Christ on the cross.
In every place we see new life and hope,
may we remember Christ's resurrection.
You are the God of life, death, and life
again—our eternal hope.
Amen.

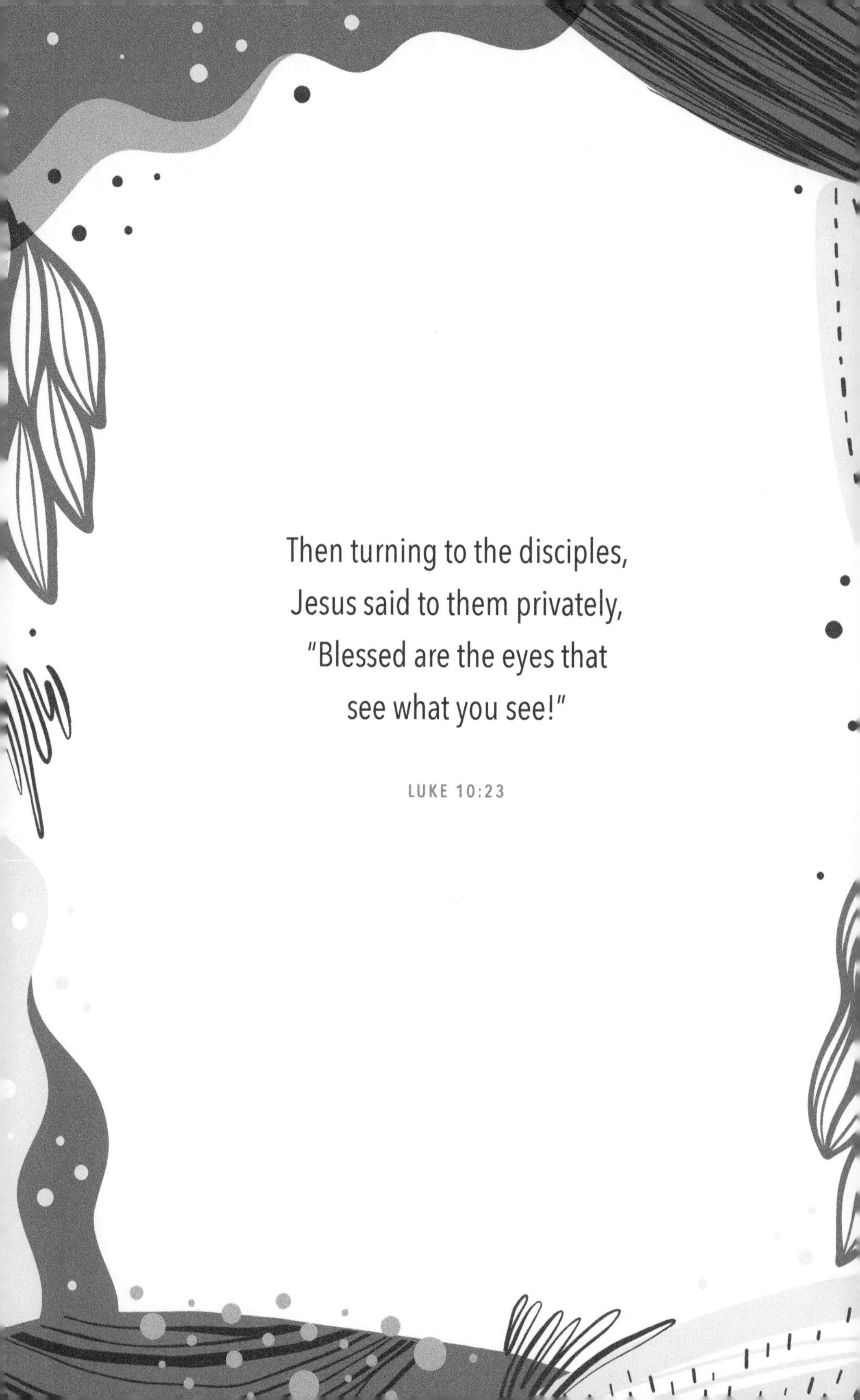

Then turning to the disciples,
Jesus said to them privately,
"Blessed are the eyes that
see what you see!"

LUKE 10:23

A TWO-DIMENSIONAL EXISTENCE

The problem with mirrors is that they never tell the whole truth. They tell a two-dimensional story. They reflect, not represent. If they are warped, they tell a warped story. If they are scratched, they show a world with a line drawn through it. They can't tell the whole truth because they are designed to show you a representation.

Jesus spent a lot of time with people helping them see the world as God had created it. He wanted them to see God represented in the world, in the mustard seed, in the woman who gave her last coin, in the birds of the air. He wanted them to see living, breathing, tangible expressions of God's presence rather than shallow reflections offered by many of the spiritual teachers of his time. He would have understood what Voltaire meant when he said, "God made man in his own image, and man returned the favor." When we have the eyes to see, we see where God is present and what God is really doing rather than what we want to see.

Most of us live reflective lives. We reflect the people we admire. We reflect achievements that others reward. We reflect the behaviors we see in our friends. We act as mirrors.

It shocks us, then, when we see people who are unique in the world. We call them trailblazers, mavericks, iconoclasts, crazy. But if we look more closely, we discover that they are the most real.

When we encounter extraordinary people who are fully themselves, without concern for mirroring anyone else to earn approval, we have the sense that we are in the presence of someone powerful. We feel their sacredness. We feel God coming through. Most powerfully, we feel seen by them because we have the sense that God is looking back at us through them.

Jesus was that clear embodiment of God's spirit in human form. Jesus was the best example we have seen of God's true presence manifest in the world. But what Jesus was saying to his disciples and to the rest of us is to look at each other with the eyes of faith. Find God in each other. You will know it when you see the uniqueness of their being bravely shining through.

REFLECT

How would you talk about the difference between being reflecting and being authentic?

How does being authentic actually free you to be unique?

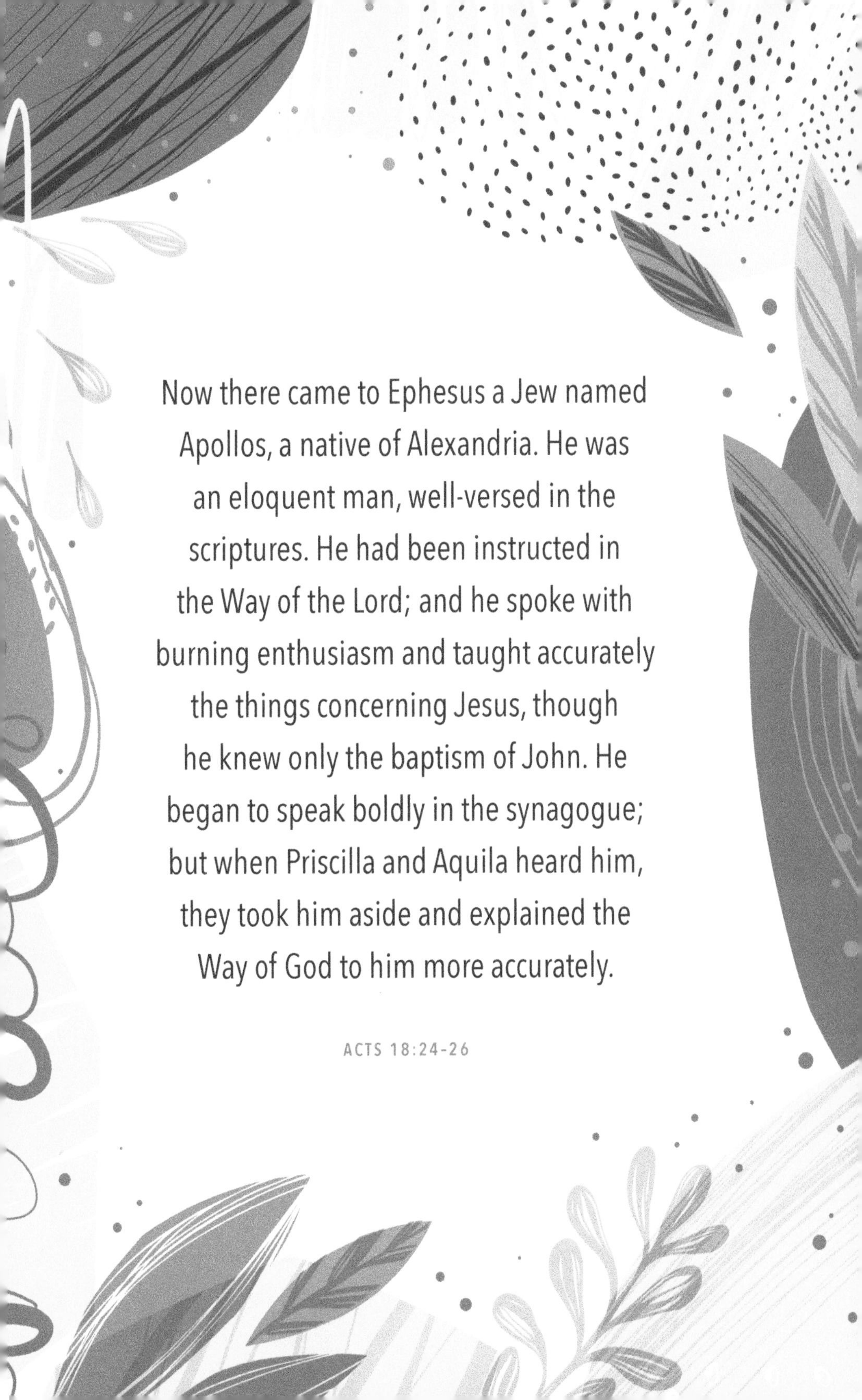

Now there came to Ephesus a Jew named Apollos, a native of Alexandria. He was an eloquent man, well-versed in the scriptures. He had been instructed in the Way of the Lord; and he spoke with burning enthusiasm and taught accurately the things concerning Jesus, though he knew only the baptism of John. He began to speak boldly in the synagogue; but when Priscilla and Aquila heard him, they took him aside and explained the Way of God to him more accurately.

ACTS 18:24-26

WISE INVESTMENTS

I was lucky enough to be raised by some wonderful women who invested in shaping me into the woman I am today. My aunt is certainly one. We spent many hours in her kitchen, me sitting on the counter watching her cook while we talked. She would take me to the plant nursery and let me roam among the flowers. She would put me on the back of her bicycle in a child seat, and we would ride around her neighborhood. She taught me to work hard, plan ahead, wear my seat belt, and always brush my teeth.

She would also call me out. When I waited until the last minute to finish a project, she would lecture me about procrastination. When I was rude to others, she would correct my behavior. Perhaps you had a similar "aunt" in your life? I hope you did.

We need these wise women. In this passage from Acts, did you just love the last line? " . . . *but when Priscilla and Aquila heard him, they took him aside and explained the Way of God to him more accurately."* I think I have had that same lecture. We all learn by doing, but we need people courageous enough to tell us when we are simply full of it.

We need Priscillas and Aquilas in our lives. They shape our dreams. They calm our fears. They provoke our imaginations. They correct our limiting beliefs. They pray for our happiness.

Consider the investments others have made in you. Consider taking a moment to thank them. Then consider how you are paying that forward. Are you investing in other people's wholeness?

If I read the Bible correctly, it seems like a key idea that keeps repeating is simply: Investing in *people* is a far better bet than investing in *things.*

REFLECT

Who were the women in your life who invested in you?

How are you living the lessons they taught you?

CLOSING PRAYER

Lord God,
I give you thanks for the wise women,
the ones who don't take nonsense from
anyone, the ones who know what needs
to be done, the ones who understand
that love is sometimes tough. May I,
in my accumulating years, begin to
recognize that I can become one, too.
Amen.

Keep on doing the things
that you have learned and
received and heard and
seen in me, and the God of
peace will be with you.

PHILIPPIANS 4:9

PRACTICE MAKES PERFECT

Much of life requires practice and repetition. When I first learned to fly airplanes, I had to practice maneuvers over and over. My instructor would demonstrate them, and then I had to try. My head understood what to do, but often my body would do something crazy. I would overcorrect on a turn or almost turn a stall into a spin. I would know my radio calls but then bumble them when I keyed up my mic to call the tower. It took months of practicing over and over to finally feel like I could competently fly.

Adults learn through practice and repetition. Think back to the days when you were first learning to drive. Likely, your parent would sit beside you and go over and over what you needed to know to be safe. Or remember when you baked your first cake. My first cake was like a sunken brick—we used it to patch holes in our driveway. But my second cake was better. My third cake was really good. Then I decided I could just buy them from a bakery and save myself the stress!

We can't be prepared for everything in life, but life flows more smoothly when we find good teachers, learn everything we can, and practice often. One way to understand the Bible is as a series of stories of spiritual teachers offering new lessons, people learning, and then experiencing transformation through practicing. Philippians 4:9 reminds us that much of the life of faith is simply practicing living as much in the spirit of Jesus as we can. Some days will be great. Some days we will fail.

I suppose that is why we call it "practicing our faith." We learn by doing.

REFLECT

What practices help you most in your faith journey?

What would you like to practice more?

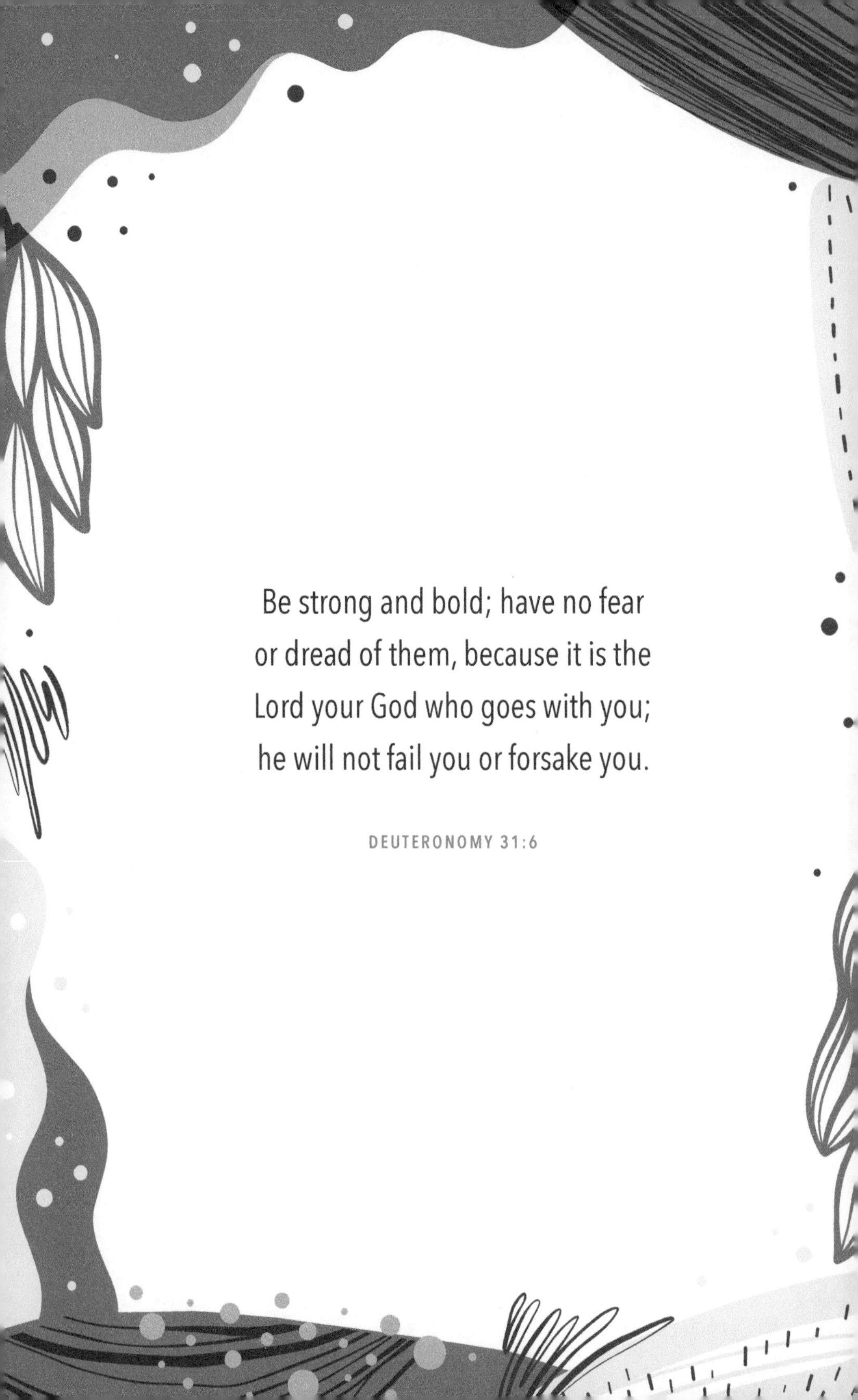

Be strong and bold; have no fear
or dread of them, because it is the
Lord your God who goes with you;
he will not fail you or forsake you.

DEUTERONOMY 31:6

SUBTLE CHANGE

I wear clothes that are either black or white. Sometimes I wear jeans that are blue. But that's it. I don't vary my wardrobe much. I started doing this a few years ago because I was traveling so much that I needed to be able to "grab and go." I needed the safety of being able to mix an outfit without the fear that I forgot the matching shoes or the necklace that made the whole outfit come together.

I like wearing black and white. I like the simplicity.

But last week, a woman at an event told me that I needed to wear bright green. Or I could wear pink, she said, but it had to be a fuchsia pink, not a pale pink. The blood left my face, and my palms began to sweat. "What?" I thought. "Mess up my wardrobe with color?"

Our challenge today is to discover how subtle changes can open us to new perceptions of what is possible—even preferred—in our life. Deuteronomy says be bold and strong. God is with you. No matter what happens, God will never leave or forsake you. That is good news when we are trying something new. Change can be scary. But change is essential to life. If we don't change, we stagnate. We stop growing. We stop becoming who God dreams for us to be.

A friend of mine once said, "Our world is filled with so many beautiful colors. Have you noticed? Thousands of shades of red and blue and green. It's like an endless emission of creativity and we get to use them in so many amazing ways! It seems to me that we should relish them all." That had never occurred to me until she said that. Sometimes it takes a friend to help us see new possibilities right in front of us. Sometimes we need such friends to accompany us as we embrace how those new possibilities can change us.

I'm considering the advice of the woman who suggested I embrace color in my wardrobe. Gray is a color, right? Maybe I will try gray . . .

REFLECT

What changes in your life are you struggling with right now?

What small step could you take today that would help you move closer to embracing change?

CLOSING PRAYER

God, grant me the serenity to accept
the things I cannot change,
courage to change the things I can,
And wisdom to know the difference.

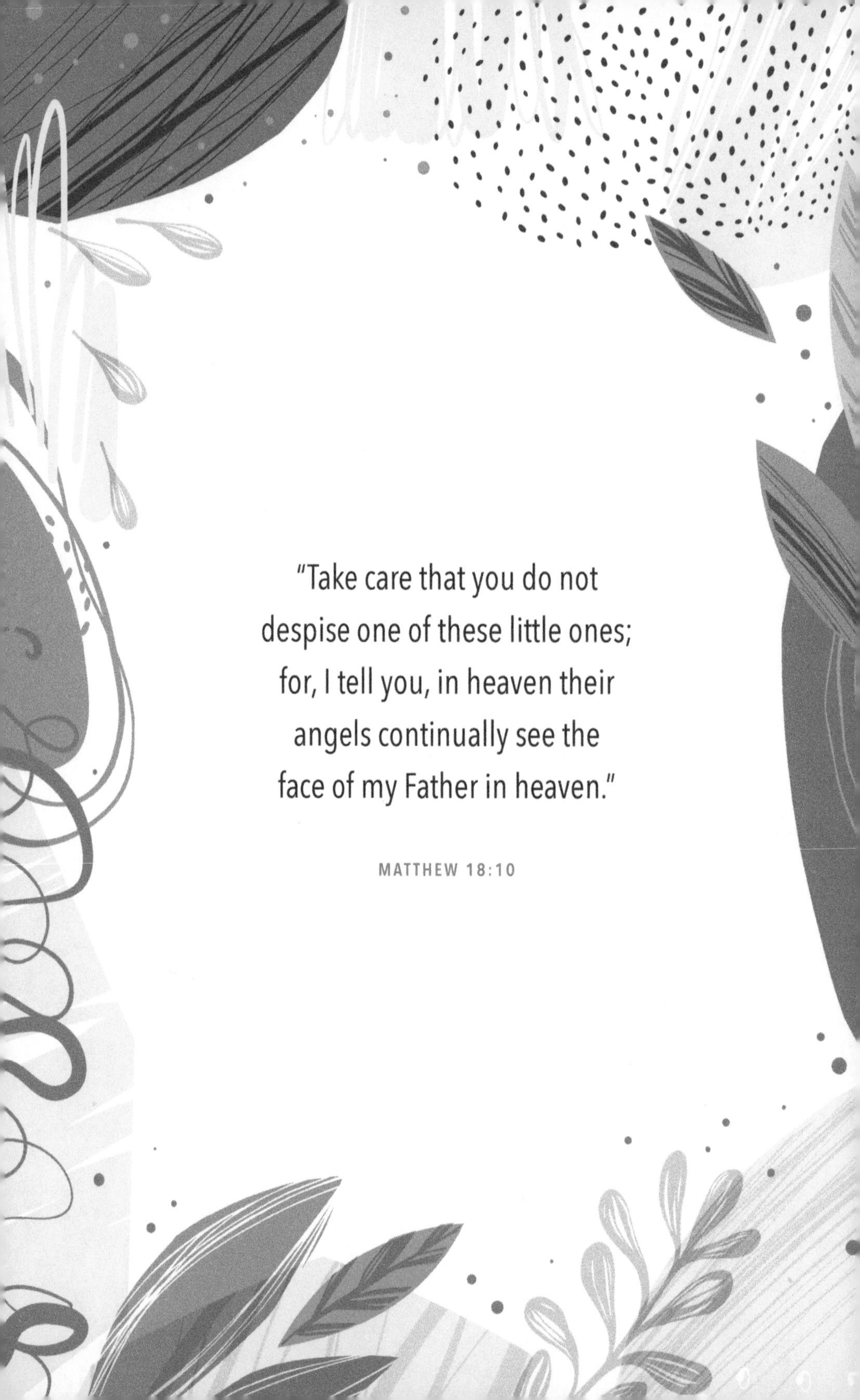

"Take care that you do not despise one of these little ones; for, I tell you, in heaven their angels continually see the face of my Father in heaven."

MATTHEW 18:10

THE SIMPLE JOY OF PLAYING

I have forgotten how to play. I sit in front of Legos and toy cars and stuffed animals, and I freeze. What should I do with these objects? Organize them? Color-code and label them? Store them away? This past weekend my two-year-old buddy Ethan came to my rescue.

Ethan and I got to spend a few hours together playing, and he taught me. We would stack cans on top of each other into a big tower, and then he would get this mischievous grin on his face. With a swift swing of his arm, the cans would go flying across the room, and he would squeal with joy. I was thinking, "Look at the mess!" He was thinking, "What fun! Let's stack them all and do it again!" Then we played with Play-Doh. I created a perfect ball. He took it and smashed it into a blob. Laughing, he would hand it back to me and say, "Again, Cam! Again!" Over and over, adventure after adventure, we played our hearts out.

Then something beautiful happened to me. I found delight in his delight. I wanted to start smashing our towers and squishing our Play-Doh. I wanted to run in the yard and kick a ball and roll toy trucks through the dirt—just to feel the simple joy of playing.

The Scriptures talk about children as one of the greatest gifts from God and perhaps the purest expression of God's true essence. They are free of the burdens of having and doing too much. They simply get to be, to exist in the moment and delight in all that is before them. They make messes and don't care about when dinner will be ready. They play until they want to stop. Then they move on to the next grand adventure.

Ethan is a gift in so many ways, but I am indebted to him for teaching me that making a mess is marvelous fun and being playful is at the heart of a well-lived life.

I hope you find time to play today.

REFLECT

What could you do today that would be playful and creative?

What is the messiest part of your life that is also the most fun?

I can do all things through
him who strengthens me.

PHILIPPIANS 4:13

“MYTHING” LINKS

We are living, walking, breathing stories. Every day we are writing a new chapter of the story of our life, one that we hope will be brave, wise, and faithful. We go on quests—meeting the future in-laws, going on job interviews and grand vacations to new lands, having children (or not), accomplishing great projects—all as ways of living out the story that was born with us and in us. At the end of our life, our loved ones will tell of the story we lived. They will reflect on the difference we made, the amusing moments where we stumbled, the moments we mattered to them.

In writing to the people of Philippi, Paul was imploring them to remember to live lives reflective of God's call. It might be difficult at moments, he said. All good stories have their moments of crisis. But remember that your story is powerful because you know the love of Christ, that you can do all things through Christ who strengthens you for the journey. So live boldly, Paul said. That is what God hopes for you.

Philosopher and author Jean Houston once said, “You must realize that we are ‘mything links,’ links between the great mythic stories, the great stories of all times and places, and the playing out of those stories in everyday life.”

I love this description of the human journey. We are the tellers of stories with both our words and our lives. Consider your life. Can you remember a time when it felt like you:

- Felt the power of fire run through your veins with Prometheus?
- Held the weight of the world on your shoulders with Atlas?
- Experienced painful death and resurrection to a new life with Jesus?

Stories are the most powerful force in the world. Stories are the juice through which consciousness and culture move. As you begin this day, think about the stories that shape you, the ones you are living out now. Are they worthy of your grand quest? Are they the mything links to a brave and loving life?

The best part about your story is that you are the author. You can always rewrite it if needed.

REFLECT

Outline the story of your life from today until the end of your life. What adventures do you want to experience? What monsters could you imagine blocking your way? What lessons do you hope to learn along the way?

CLOSING PRAYER

Gracious God,
Grant me a life of grand adventure,
one where I feel the rush of
accomplishment, face the fears of
failure, meet wonderful mentors along
the way, and discover strength in myself
I never dreamed possible. I want to live
a brave and beautiful life, one guided
and inspired by you, so that in the end
I might hear your blessing: "Well done,
my good and faithful servant."
Amen.

"This is my commandment, that you love one another as I have loved you. No one has greater love than this, to lay down one's life for one's friends."

JOHN 15:12-13

MISSING WHAT MATTERS

One of the many gifts women bring into the world is that of creating deep, lasting friendships. We have a sense of sisterhood that bonds us to one another, especially in times of struggle. We don't limit our bonds only to women—we certainly extend that embrace to men—yet women seem to form the relational fabric strong enough to hold families and communities together.

This past week I had the chance to spend two days with dear friends. They welcomed me to their beautiful lake home, and we ate thoughtful, generous meals they prepared in anticipation of my arrival. Each morning, we took long walks in the woods by their home. We savored our morning coffee while watching the birds outside the kitchen window. We played together with their dog. We talked about life, our work, our heartbreak with the world. We were deeply, fully present with each other.

When I drove off at the end of our visit, I thought about how rare and precious that experience was for me. I felt healed in a way I didn't even know I needed. Only love and friendship can do that.

When Jesus said that no one has greater love than to lay down one's life for one's friend, I don't think he was advocating that we all die for each other. He was saying that love is made real when we die to our own self-centered agendas so that we can be together. When I was with my friends, they weren't busy on their phones or running errands. They laid down their busy lives and set aside the normal distractions so that we could deeply connect to one another.

I pray that you are lucky enough to spend time with people you love and that you slow down enough to be fully present with each other. We are all moving so fast these days. Our souls aren't built for this fast-food diet of technology addiction and constant motion. We are missing so much that matters.

If you have the chance, make it a priority to be present with someone today. Really see them and let them see you. If you're lucky, when you look at them, you might also catch a glimpse of God looking back.

REFLECT

Who are the friends who mean the most to you in your life? What is it about them that matters so much to you?

How are you showing up as a friend to others?

REFERENCES

Beck, Martha. "You Have Reached Your Destination." Last modified December 2017. https://marthabeck.com/2017/12/you-have-reached-your-destination.

Karpman, Stephen B. "Part 1. The '202.'" Karpman Drama Triangle. Accessed January 26, 2020. https://karpmandramatriangle.com.

Kitching, Audrey. "Facebook Update." Last modified July 13, 2018. https://www.facebook.com/TheOfficialAudreyKitching/posts/forgive-yourself-for-not-knowing-better-at-the-timeforgive-yourself-for-giving-a/10156273333346023.

Loyola Press. "Peace Prayer of Saint Francis." Accessed January 26, 2020. https://www.loyolapress.com/our-catholic-faith/prayer/traditional-catholic-prayers/saints-prayers/peace-prayer-of-saint-francis.

"Microaggression." Dictionary.com. Accessed January 26, 2020. https://www.dictionary.com/browse/microaggression.

Rowling, J. K. "The Fringe Benefits of Failure." Last modified June 2008. https://www.ted.com/talks/jk_rowling_the_fringe_benefits_of_failure.

Rowling, J. K. *Very Good Lives*. New York: Little, Brown and Company, 2015.

Shapiro, Fred R. "Who Wrote the Serenity Prayer?" The Chronicle of Higher Education. Last modified April 28, 2014. https://www.chronicle.com/article/Who-Wrote-the-Serenity-Prayer-/146159.

Zuckerberg, Randi. "Randi Zuckerberg's Remarkably Simple Advice for Achieving Your Daily Goals." Last modified May 15, 2018. https://qz.com/1274601/randi-zuckerbergs-advice-for-achieving-your-life-goals-pick-three.

INDEX

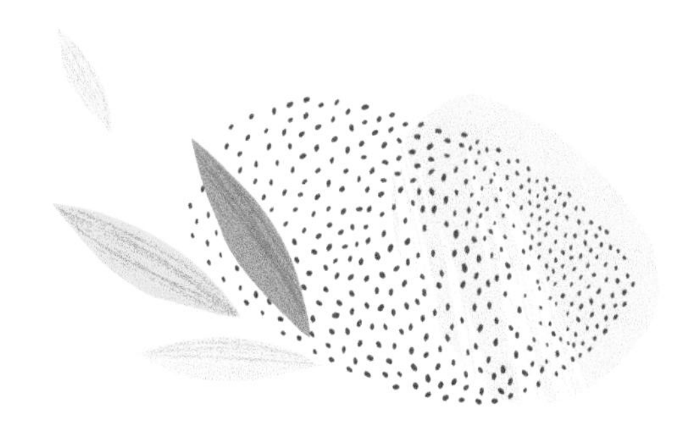

ABOUT THE AUTHOR

Rev. Cameron Trimble is a pastor and denominational leader in the United Church of Christ, an organizational consultant, a frequent keynoter on national speaking circuits, a pilot, and an author of a number of books about faith and leadership. She writes an (almost) daily meditation you can find at www.pilotingfaith.org. She also serves as the CEO of Convergence Network (www.convergenceus.org).

For more, see www.camerontrimble.com.

Public contact information:
facebook.com/cameron.trimble
twitter.com/cambtrim
linkedin.com/in/camerontrimble